AGGRESSIVELY HUMAN

"A compelling read about the evolution of a man who confronted challenges and came out the other side."

—Neil Strauss, Ten-Time *New York Times* Best-Selling Author

"I read *Aggressively Human* as a senator, a feminist, and a football fan. It's a bold, and sometimes brutal account of what it takes to survive and thrive."

—Gloria Romero, Former California Senate Majority Leader

"Ride shotgun with Steve as he keeps it real in *Aggressively Human*."

—Eric Dickerson, Pro Football Hall of Fame & Raiders Teammate

"To call Steve a peaceful warrior would not be too far a stretch. *Aggressively Human* is refreshingly authentic."

—Dr. Ronald Stolberg, Former Psychologist for *Survivor*

"*Aggressively Human* is a brutally honest, unflinching self-portrait of a man who must reconcile his killer instinct in pro football, TV's most famous reality competition show, and the cutthroat business world with his innate kindness. Steve Wright offers a heartfelt lesson for anyone who is interested in living a better, more compassionate life."

—Ann Yih Johnson, Former CBS News Executive

"*Aggressively Human* is the perfect title for a book so full of passionate punch and honest heart."

—Randall Wallace, Writer of *Braveheart*

"*Aggressively Human* is a humorous, self-deprecating look behind the scenes of professional football and into the soul of a 'just win, baby' competitor. Don't let his good looks fool you!"

—Dr. Rob Huizenga, Former Physician for Raiders and *Biggest Loser*

"Steve rose to the occasion and beyond, as does *Aggressively Human*."

—Harry Pierce, Former President of the Home Depot

"*Aggressively Human* reveals honest and unfiltered insights from the locker room, Nicaraguan jungle, Olympics, and Steve's soul to discover the balance we all seek."

—David Hoy, PhD, Author, Psychologist, Executive Coach

"Steve has a kind soul that shines through in his memoir, *Aggressively Human*."

—Sean Poynter, Former SUP Surfing World Champion

"This gentle giant offers up a fun-loving journey along with deep revelations about living fully and uncovering your best self. He brings us inside the NFL, where we would otherwise not have access to go. What a treat to be in the room where it happened!"

—John C. McGinley, Actor, *Platoon*, *Scrubs*

"I would gladly go to war with Steve anytime. You will understand why once you read *Aggressively Human*."

—Steve Beuerlein, Super Bowl Champion, Pro Bowl and Raiders Teammate

Aggressively Human
Discovering Humanity in the NFL, Reality TV, and Life

by Steve Wright
with Lizzy Wright

© Copyright 2023 Steve Wright

ISBN 979-8-88824-156-1

All rights reserved. No part of this publication may be reproduced, stored in a retrieval system, or transmitted in any form or by any means—electronic, mechanical, photocopy, recording, or any other—except for brief quotations in printed reviews, without the prior written permission of the author.

Photo Credits: Dallas Cowboys Football Club, Ltd., Raiders Football Club, LLC

Published by

3705 Shore Drive
Virginia Beach, VA 23455
800-435-4811
www.koehlerbooks.com

AGGRESSIVELY HUMAN

Discovering Humanity in the NFL, Reality TV, and Life

STEVE WRIGHT

with Lizzy Wright

VIRGINIA BEACH
CAPE CHARLES

For those who live in full color and light the way for others.

"A human is not a being, he is a becoming, he is an ongoing process - nothing is fixed. You can be whichever way you want to be."
—Sadhguru

TABLE OF CONTENTS

DISCLAIMERS ... 7

INTRODUCTION: KILLER ... 9

CHAPTER 1: THE CAREFREE COWBOY ... 13

CHAPTER 2: BORN A BEAST ... 42

CHAPTER 3: TESTING GROUND ... 59

CHAPTER 4: GAME TIME ... 67

CHAPTER 5: GLORIFIED RENEGADES ... 80

CHAPTER 6: TIME TO GROW ... 127

CHAPTER 7: OPPORTUNITY KNOCKS ... 154

CHAPTER 8: THE SEEKER ... 163

CHAPTER 9: FLOW LIKE WATER ... 197

CHAPTER 10: FORWARD MOMENTUM ... 202

ACKNOWLEDGMENTS ... 206

REFERENCES ... 208

DISCLAIMERS

Some names and identifying details have been changed to protect the privacy of individuals. This work contains language that may be offensive to some readers. It is included to reflect what was said and done before movements that have evolved the collective consciousness. No disrespect is intended.

INTRODUCTION

KILLER

His teammates called him Killer. He earned this nickname in the wrecking yard of football. When he was in the zone and ready for war, it was best to steer clear.

An All-Pro lineman for the Los Angeles Raiders, Killer was a battle-tested gladiator known for excessively taped and padded arms that felt like clubs when they rattled spines and mashed bodies. He was a perfect fit for right tackle, preferring the dirty work of demolition over dancing in the end zone. Touchdowns were too soft. He needed violent contact to feel alive.

Killer was a world away from the empathetic men who shaped me. My father and grandfather embraced everyone; even a trip to the store reinforced their connectedness. I watched them express kindness through their words and actions as they checked on workers, from deli clerks to baggers. I wanted to be one of these gentle and beloved men. Unlike Killer, they focused on the good in people, not the weakness.

However, empathy doesn't get you far on the field. There was only one spot left on the offensive line, and two people wanted it. One was Killer. The other was me. I hated that making this well-intact team would come at a price for someone else, even a guy known as Killer. But this was business. I understood how this drama could unfold as I watched it too many times. If I received the dreaded instruction to visit the front office, I was done. Any player headed in that direction during preseason was a dead man walking, head down, and about to have his dreams torn from his soul.

If I lost the spot to Killer, I would watch him from my living room couch like every other fan. Sure, I could talk about my years with the Cowboys and Colts, but my childhood dream of playing for the NFL's notorious outlaws, the Raiders, would die a fantasy.

As I suited up for the high-stakes scrimmage, my mind raced through plays and position assignments. The designs were straightforward, but the players were the wild cards. I only had four weeks of training camp with this motley crew of no-rules Raiders. That wasn't enough time to learn their on-field tendencies. Just when I thought I had a defensive lineman figured out, he surprised me.

But my biggest challenge, present for as long as I can remember, was an inside job. I had to silence my humanity on the field; there was no way around it. I needed to raise the dormant beast beneath my more peaceful nature. These mental gymnastics weren't for everyone; there was no playbook, seatbelt, or handrail. But my future in professional football depended on unearthing my alter ego.

I emerged from the locker room with Marcus Allen. He was a sleek and slender cheetah of a running back who could artfully navigate through any defense. I watched him keep the mood infectiously light with ribs for all players within earshot. I wanted to relax as well, but the risk was far too great for me. Marcus already had a Super Bowl Most Valuable Player (MVP) award under his belt. He had nothing to worry about that morning. As we were about to join our position groups, he paused and grabbed my face mask, saying, "Stay loose and kick ass."

I took his words to heart, needing this vote of confidence. Meanwhile, the always cool defensive end Greg Townsend sauntered by offering a grunt while a lit cigarette still hung from his mouth. Even in the trail of smoke, his cool was unmistakable.

Once I peeled off to join the other offensive linemen, Killer acknowledged my presence with an unexpected nod, catching me mid-step. I fought to keep my balance. I couldn't let his mind games soften me. I needed to flick the switch, letting my animal instincts take care of the rest. It was time to get ugly.

I paced like a caged animal on the sideline as Killer joined the starting lineup. The call was made for thirty-six sweep right. This play would highlight his skill in blocking off the outside linebacker to allow Marcus a clean sweep around the right end. With the camera crew positioned to capture whatever wasn't observed by the naked eye, the cadre of coaches could meticulously dissect each movement deep into the night. Every step and hand placement would be under a microscope.

Killer coiled into his stance with his clubs cocked, preparing to launch off the line. At the snap, he did his job, but not before coming off the ball late, which had to be captured on film. There was a glimmer of hope for me.

After the first quarter, I had a chance to prove my worth as I replaced Killer on the field. I blew past, refusing to make eye contact. My humanity was a distant memory. I was locked, loaded, and ready to explode off the line like a missile carrying a heavy payload. Seeing myself as a weapon of war helped get me in the right frame of mind. At the snap, I overwhelmed the outside linebacker to signal that Killer should be a bygone era. I fought to be quicker off the ball, applying better technique and offering more versatility: a new, improved model for the offensive line.

By my third play of the scrimmage, I was in the flow. The Super Bowl MVP quarterback, Jim Plunkett, called for a screen pass to Marcus. I pass-blocked my guy, dropping back as he rushed in, fighting for a sack. I went for his legs to bring his hands down, leaving a clear throwing lane as the ball floated past and landed in Marcus's hands for another first down. The chemistry of this unit was solid. Even the coaches nodded their approval.

Killer saw this, too, and wanted back in. They exchanged us the next quarter to see if he could up the ante. Now he played with controlled rage harnessed by over a decade of experience. He fought off plenty of guys like me trying to take his spot over the years. He rose to the occasion, offering a pro-bowl-worthy performance, dominating the next series. Even Plunkett gave him a solid back slap for providing strong protection from future Hall of Famer Howie Long. If Killer could wall off Howie, he wasn't ready to be cut loose.

I shook my head, not wanting to concede. Neither of us was ready to go quietly that day as our unbridled aggression was on full display. As I gathered my things in the locker room after the mentally and physically exhausting scrimmage, I caught Killer watching me. I finally lowered my guard as we honored each other with a nod of respect.

There had to be another layer behind Killer's predatory bravado. I guessed that his on-field aggression was balanced out by a gentler self far out of view of the gridiron. Likewise, Killer didn't know I carried a heart full of compassion that steadied me off the field. We could see each other at that moment, but we wouldn't truly know one another for another thirty years. Meanwhile, one of us would be rewarded that day—not for our humanity but for our inhumanity on the field.

I left the locker room asking myself the same question I had struggled with for years: could I navigate the uneasy intersection between aggression and empathy and not lose myself? The answer to this question would determine the course of my career and my life.

CHAPTER 1

THE CAREFREE COWBOY

Everyone around me vanished. My world went from near-constant action to an abrupt silence. Cowboys training camp was over. The team and the front office prepared for a must-win season opener while my fate hung in the balance, sequestered in a Dallas hotel, waiting for the last few roster spots to be decided. I was a man caught between worlds for the first of many times. I resigned to pacing around my barren room, anticipating a call that would either send me back to Minneapolis in search of a sales job or into the Cowboys' locker room to live out a dream.

At the start of camp, I was one of one hundred and twenty top athletes attempting to secure five, possibly six, spots on the roster to scrounge like a beggar for momentary playing time. The odds were stacked against me since the Cowboys picked up a first- and third-round draft pick to fill out their 1981 offensive line. Given these high selections, an underweight, undrafted rookie out of Northern Iowa was an unlikely pick. But I clung to one sliver of hope during my solitary confinement: the Cowboys were known for finding players passed over by other teams. Could I be their diamond in the rough? I wasn't even all-conference in college, so my diamond was far from flawless, but anything was possible.

While at camp, I shared a modest dorm room with five other rookies from all walks of life: three beefy farm boys, a street-smart city kid, and a squeaky-clean Bible-thumper. It was an interesting psychological experiment to observe how each player handled the intensity. One of the rookies snuck out for a quick reefer break each night while another read his Bible in his tighty-whities until lights out. As for me, those training camp nights were among a handful in my life when I cried under my pillow as exhaustion and fear collided. It was a tiresome mental exercise to keep the concerns at bay. In the quiet of the night, with my mind as my sole companion, I wondered if I was enough of a warrior to make the team.

I learned to fear the prankster who summoned players to see Head Coach Tom Landry in addition to providing daily wake-up calls. If he asked me to see Coach and bring my playbook, I would be done and released from the facility by the top of the hour. I had the misfortune of watching this nightmare-inducing scene up close five times as each of my roommates met this fate by the fourth week. Then, as the last rookie on my block, the grim reaper began messing with me. He would bang on my door, bust it open, and shout, "Get up, get your playbook, and get over to... practice right now," slamming the door and laughing his way down the hall to shake up the last few hopefuls.

With the first adrenaline rush of the day behind me, I moved on to the dreaded mandatory weigh-ins. I loathed that all-too-honest scale. I was a meager 258 pounds and couldn't afford to give up an ounce. But most days, I lost eight pounds despite holding off on bathroom stops and loading my short pockets with all the spare change I could find. It was a Weight Watchers wet dream but my daily nightmare.

A good four of those fleeting pounds were rung out of my towel after each practice. The rest was a consequence of insanely high caloric burn. To regain some ground each night, I relied on double supreme pizzas from a truck wisely parked outside our dorms like clockwork just before curfew. Those pizza boxes served as my last sight before bed and first discernable image each morning with empty cardboard teetering on my chest. It was a vicious cycle as the daily conditioning test of ten forty-yard dash sprints worked through my reserves before nine o'clock in the morning. But I still enjoyed these assessments because this is where I excelled with the lowest accumulated time among the offensive linemen. Lucky for me, I was born to run . . . just a bit faster than a dump truck full of pizza boxes.

While the weigh-ins were concerning, the chart next to the scale induced panic. I could break out in a cold sweat just thinking about it, but I couldn't afford to lose more water weight. The posted printout held the names of all the rookies vying for a spot on the roster. As the weeks wore on, it resembled a heavily redacted government document with thick Sharpie lines through players' names. Even though they were my competition, most were warriors who departed far too soon. I suppose they were now back in their hometowns, wondering what could've been. There was a good chance that I was about to join them.

All the time to overanalyze was frustrating as I nearly bore a trench pacing the length of my hotel room. It was two straight days of only outgoing calls reaching out to family and friends for emotional strength. Finally, in the forty-sixth hour, I received one inbound ring that pierced the air like a three-alarm fire. I didn't have time to panic. I just grabbed it and pulled in a shallow breath.

"Steve, it's Gil." Gil Brandt was the Cowboys' director of player personnel and the dealer of my fate.

I swallowed hard past the nervous lump lodged in my throat.

"We appreciate your effort. You worked your tail off, and we thank you," he said, pausing for effect.

It sounded like I was on my way out. The sweating started, and my heart careened into a stomach full of lasagna.

Then Gil's tone switched from somber to joyous within an instant. "Grab your playbook and bring it over . . . you're going to need it. Congratulations, Steve, you're now a Dallas Cowboy."

I lost all control as my body launched onto the bed and across to the adjoining twin, which collapsed under my weight. I could only imagine how this sounded on the other end of the phone line.

"Steve, you okay?" probed Gil as the sounds of shuffling paper abruptly stopped on his end of the line.

I held onto the phone like an oxygen mask, breathlessly bellowing, "Sir, yes, sir," as if I had just entered the military. I was too stunned by the news and my collapse to say anything else.

Gil offered a laugh, wrapping up the call. Once the receiver hit the phone cradle, I busted into the hallway like a freed animal, shouting as the familiar taste of exertion touched my tongue. I had never savored a triumph so sweet, and I was hooked.

Cowboys Rookie Year, 1981

I enjoyed plenty of Cowboys' perks in those early days: some minor and many a ton of fun. One night, I grabbed a rental car from the Cowboys lot with the fifth-round draft pick from Tennessee, Danny Spradlin. We had nothing in common except for our absolute live-or-die love of football and passion for weightlifting.

He was built like Mr. Universe. His V-shaped upper body had muscles stacked on muscles with jacked biceps that prevented his fingers from touching his nose. One day, I spotted him doing curls and watched his glasses slide down his beak. After he finished his set, he leaned into me and sheepishly asked, "Wud ya push my glasses back up? I can't reach." His twang was unmistakable, like molasses mixed with moonshine.

We also shared a love of beer, which was the source of our troubles one night. Having consumed a few too many cervezas in town, I was punching it home to meet the strict 11 p.m. curfew. About to blow through a yellow light, but fearing a DWI or worse, I stomped on the brakes, launching an unbuckled Danny into the windshield like a 235-pound crash test dummy. It could've been a seatbelt advertisement with his impact spreading a spiderweb of cracks across the glass. Danny lay crumpled and motionless in the passenger seat while I entered full-fledged crisis mode.

"Holy shit," I shouted, fearing that I had just snapped the neck of this prized draft pick. I leaned over and shook Danny's leg to revive him.

After a few seconds of silence that felt like an eternity, he raised his bulletproof noggin', shook his broken glasses loose, and gave me a blank stare as he wondered aloud, "Wud you do that for, buddy?"

I was convinced he would punch my lights out next. But this beast of a man turned into a softie off the field, making me appreciate him even more. Mother of all things sacred, I was relieved that he was okay. I drove the rest of the way home, hanging out the window to see past the remains of the windshield. And as I pulled into the lot just shy of curfew, one of the Cowboys staff sauntered by, stopping dead in his tracks to survey the damage. "Nice work, fuckin' Rook!" he shouted as he shook his head in disbelief. Not surprisingly, I wasn't permitted another loaner, and the other players had one less car at their disposal, leading to some locker room grumbling. I had a deep hole to climb out of, given my early deviation from model Cowboy behavior.

Weeks later, when the season was in full swing, an incident on the field left me wondering if the windshield had a lasting impact. We were playing in St. Louis, with me and Danny rounding out the punt team. We raced down the field to blow up the aptly named receiver, Stump Mitchell, when he waved his arms for the fair catch. I slowed down while Danny had other plans. Of the 65,000 fans, players, and ball boys in attendance, only Danny ignored the wave. He was a heat-seeking missile that launched into Stump's chest with such brutal force that he almost separated his head from his body. It was the first of many times that I would see an ambulance on the field. Stump required some serious medical attention. Meanwhile, Danny was ejected from the game for violating the fair-catch rule and nearly publicly dismembering another human being on live television.

But perhaps the desire to hit fresh meat was to blame when Danny leveled Stump. We had just completed a grueling training camp with two daily practices hitting the same guys play after play. Each session would last two and a half hours, followed by weightlifting before dinner and another two hours of meetings before bed. The endless routine was bound to drive any sane man crazy.

The lifting was set up in a large cage designed to prevent theft, but it left us feeling like zoo animals. We were fully on display as the public crowded four deep to watch us train. They captured every barbell drop, ball scratch, and nose pick. But we never complained about our practices being open to the public since plenty of girls joined the crowd hoping to snare a Cowboy.

There was also a lineup of grade-school boys outside the locker room vying to carry our helmets over the four weeks of camp. Their beat-up old bikes, dirty knees, and eager energy always brought a smile to my face. While I never got this opportunity as a kid, I saw myself in their hungry eyes as they wanted in on the daily ritual of lugging our helmets. We would exit the locker room for the long walk to the field, and these boys would be ready to go. They would have their bikes lined up like airport cabbies, facing the field, all smiles and extended arms as they called out our names.

My first year, I chose Antonio because he appeared to be the underdog. He was the smallest kid of the bunch, but his heart was twice as big as the others. I chose wisely. He was as reliable as sunrise and sunset—a true hustler with unsurpassed energy that motored his little legs no matter the hour. A few times during camp, his whole family came by to watch their prideful son at his summer dream job. At the final camp practice, with his family waiting by the fence, I offered my genuine gratitude for their son and his diligence. I deliberately stood within earshot so Antonio could absorb the compliments, too. He smiled a little wider and stood a bit taller as I referred to him as a teammate. I never thought I would see Antonio again, and I wanted to send him off on a high note.

Coincidentally, a man approached me a few years ago, cradling a baby boy with two five-year-old twins in tow. He introduced himself as Antonio, my rookie-year helmet carrier. Imagine my surprise, followed by the big smile that spread across my face. As he spoke, I was overwhelmed with emotions, hearing how my attention and words of encouragement lifted him. Now I was the one being fed and standing taller after hearing what the relationship, nearly thirty-five years ago, meant to him. The ripple effect of good deeds was profound. Antonio explained how the camp experience elevated him and ultimately made him a better father to his three sons. It was a powerful reminder that a little extra time and encouragement can go a long way. It also reinforced that expressing compassion was a necessary complement to the aggression that dominated my life on the field.

As a young rookie, I needed my share of encouragement back then too. I was in the presence of two Super Bowl MVPs, Randy White and Harvey Martin, among a cast of other remarkable athletes. Harvey was a man among men—a big-bodied, baritone stud that you'd hear coming long before he arrived. And once he showed up, he received nothing but respect. I would've done just about anything he asked, except for one thing I discovered when my folks made the trek to check on me at camp. They joined the crowd for the evening weightlift viewing when I heard Harvey grunt and spout, "Holy shit, check her out."

Naturally, a few of us wheeled around to look, and I was mortified to watch them eyeing my mom. I had to snuff their thoughts fast, stand up, and be counted. With as much tact as I could muster, I stammered, "Come on now, guys, that's my mom!"

Harvey released a belly laugh. "No way, Rook, my bad." Then he racked his weights, wiped the stream of sweat from his eyes, and kept moving.

After practice, I brought Harvey and a few others over to meet my parents. I worried how this scene would unfold, given the incident in the weight cage, but the guys were only kind and loving toward my parents. It dawned on me that maybe some of these professionals also grappled with the uneasy intersection of life in football and beyond the turf. For the remainder of my time with the Cowboys, I shared a solid bond with Harvey, born out of the most awkward moment.

Mom at Cowboys Training Camp, 1981

The day I truly earned the star on my Cowboys' helmet is etched into my memory like cave art. In many of the one-on-one practice drills, I matched up with Harvey, who still enjoyed messing with me. He put on a façade of going easy, but once we made contact, he turned it on as a hardened professional. I was violently tossed aside, with Harvey well-positioned to take out the quarterback. But that afternoon, I snapped and went full-on rabid dog. With fists locked on face masks and in a stalemate, we hammered away until we hit the ground, kicking up dust like a Western shootout. Within seconds, other players jumped in and separated us to avoid further escalation and possible injury. But it wasn't over. As we headed to the weight cage for the nightly lift, Harvey jogged up, threw his club arm around my neck, and yanked me in close. "You're all right, Rook. You earned my respect today." This warrior code was a world away from my everyday life. Where else would uncontrolled rage be a badge of honor? I still had a lot to understand about the mind-bending world of football.

During my first year with the Cowboys, I learned additional lessons, including the importance of always arriving early. I soon discovered that the coaching staff embraced Vince Lombardi's philosophy: if you were on time for practice or a meeting, you were already fifteen minutes late. Basically, get your ass there early for everything, no exceptions. The first time I was late to a meeting by a mere ten seconds, Coach closed the door in my face as I ran to grab the knob. I was so close that I could make out the wood fibers of the door and even smell the varnish. This was coupled with the permanent mental imprint of Coach Landry's head drop with disappointment and a subsequent one-hundred-dollar fine. I would've taken a penalty ten times that amount to prevent letting down Coach. Now I would have my ass chewed out. And I dreaded further fallout when it came to playing-time decisions. There was nothing worse than irritating the legendary Coach Landry, who, while a man of few words, ran a tight ship.

How lucky was I to start my NFL career with one of the most

successful coaches of all time? Landry was a coaching god. When he commanded the room at the start of a meeting, it would be dead silent to convey the utmost respect. Then he would zero in on a few select points regarding an upcoming game but never carried on with the rah-rah crap. While he appeared stern with his tight lips, he was quite soft-spoken, never raising his voice on or off the field. In fact, he would carry a megaphone during practice. If someone screwed up and he needed to yell, he just spoke into the amplifier or delegated the barking to the closest assistant. The only negative was having him set the bar so high for every subsequent leader during my career. No one came close.

Despite my deep respect for Coach, I still managed to screw up again. But, the second time I was late, it scared me straight for the rest of my career . . . and life, I kid you not. I was leaving my house to meet the team for our game flight to Philly and realized there was a decent chance I would miss the plane. It was a monumental rookie mistake, and I was in such a panic that I floored it from my house until I blew into the Dallas Fort Worth airport. Everything blurred as I passed cars on the shoulder and drove through stoplights with a mere tap of the brakes. With a death grip on the wheel, I didn't lift my foot off the gas during a twenty-minute fast and furious freeway ride. Soaked in sweat, I hit the airport. Not literally, but close.

We had a separate parking area just off the tarmac for our Cowboys' branded jet. As I came skidding around the corner, I was relieved that our plane was on the ground, yet there was not a soul in sight. I still had a chance of making it, but not without being dressed down in front of everyone. Now the slow-acting poison of dread was taking hold. I bolted up the stairs, tucking my dress shirt in as I lunged through the door. As I rounded the corner, I couldn't avoid the cool, calm, and impeccably dressed Coach Landry. He looked through me as if I didn't exist. I remember thinking I would never make it off the bench at this rate. I lowered my head like a dog who had eaten his owner's favorite shoes and kept moving.

I scurried through the curtain and into the player's seating section with my eyes glued to the carpet, where I was rightfully met with a host of catcalls and lewd remarks. Just as I took the last seat across from the bathrooms, the crew closed the doors, and off we went. To this day, I still wake up in a sweat from reoccurring nightmares of being late for practice, a meeting, or a game. It was a painful lesson that forever altered my behavior. It was also an important reminder that I needed to show my respect to be a valued part of the team.

The Cerebral Coach, Tom Landry

While I discovered a surefire way to piss off the coaches with my tardiness, another player managed to one-up me. The Cowboys were known to have the NFL's thickest and most complicated playbook. It was our bible and considered the key to learning all about the team and how we operated. I may have been a little haphazard with some things—but never the playbook. When it rode in the passenger seat of my convertible, I secured it with the seat belt. Well, I should have. That first year with the Cowboys, I got to know one guy who regretted not taking more precautions.

Before a morning meeting, the rookie scrambled into the locker room, flustered and bear-hugging the remains of a playbook full of tread marks. I surveyed the oil and dirt plastering his hands and knees and pictured him playing twister in an intersection. While none of us could imagine his plight, we couldn't control our laughter. He was a straitlaced, no-frills introvert who was seriously struggling with the mess he created.

Once he got to his seat and attempted to flatten a few rough corners of the remains, he confessed that many more pages were strewn across the highway. He left our team bible on the roof of his car. Once he saw the binder go airborne on the highway, the disaster truly took flight as it vomited a steady stream of pages into the wind. It was a full-on Category 4 mess when he turned around and pulled over near the shredded binder. He watched helplessly as cars and semitrucks pummeled his playbook beyond recognition. Without concern for his life, he bolted into the middle of rush-hour traffic and dropped onto all fours. He tried to collect whatever he could despite the honks and foul suggestions on where he should go, namely Hell, all while begging God to help him.

Sure, I felt terrible for him, but that didn't stop me from scrambling into the meeting room to grab the best seat. It would be an entertaining start to the session as this sacrificial lamb would be brutally filleted to hammer home the importance of the team bible. It was a memorable start with plenty of stifled laughter, but he lived to fight another day and probably kept his playbook in a safe after that disaster.

While the rookies didn't make life easy for the Cowboys staff, I discovered that the coaching crew surrounded themselves with the best people to help optimize their team. Coach Landry brought in Dr. Bob Ward, a PhD in biomechanics and strength training. He was a powerhouse of a man: physically, mentally, and emotionally tough. He knew how to get the most power, speed, and agility out of every player. He also possessed the innate sense of knowing when to push and let up as he mastered this delicate tightrope.

Bob was decades ahead of other strength coaches in the league due to the depth of his knowledge and creativity. He incorporated Bruce Lee's partner, Dan Inosanto, who taught the offensive and defensive line hand-to-hand combat with quickness, strikes, and slaps. He also employed deprivation tanks to relax our minds while watching our opponents on video as we floated in blackness. It was no coincidence that in addition to the best coaches, equipment, and ideas, we also had a high winning percentage on the field.

During the 1981 season, another rookie was red-hot, picking off everything thrown in his direction and consequently making the Pro Bowl as a cornerback. I loved this guy, and so did the news media. He was a fun-loving, team-oriented player who deserved the shirt off my back if he needed it. There was always an abundance of action around his locker as the media briefings consumed the space.

One day, he had a scrum of thirty reporters surrounding him, asking the same litany of questions about his amazing plays of the game. He fiddled with his pant pocket and didn't notice the sizable bag of weed that fell at their feet. I sprang to action, quickly tossing a shirt over the contraband. Back then, smoking marijuana was a far greater offense than it is today, and it wasn't something anyone wanted to expose to the media. Once the press departed, I asked him to hand me my shirt, and he just about shit himself when he saw his bag. We shared a good laugh and bonding moment; we had each other's backs on and off the field. It also made me realize that he, too, needed help managing the pressures of football. Each player had different coping techniques.

One of my release valves led to far more trouble than I anticipated. Before settling on my house in north Dallas, I joined my buddies in a massive apartment complex called The Village, located within stumbling distance of a Disneyland of debauchery on Greenville Avenue. While we were all gainfully employed, we lived large and wild as hell, with too many temptations within reach. Honestly, we didn't even need to leave the complex to make lasting memories and, as it turns out, endure a nightmare, too.

There were about 5,000 young professionals in the complex, full of energy, and all singing from the same hymn book. With thirty pools strewn throughout the grounds and a carefree crowd, it was a playground for misbehavior. We had a reputation for our crazy pool parties, and another one for the books was on the docket one summer morning. It started like all its predecessors: the typical floating kegs, bar, and band with a start time of 10 a.m. and ending when the police drew their weapons. Word of the party got out fast, and attendance ballooned. Any attempts to reign in bad behavior were increasingly futile. After a few hours of partying, I sobered up and eventually split with my girlfriend to get some much-needed dinner followed by a movie. At about midnight, I jumped into my convertible to head home, roof down, no shirt or shoes, and sober as an altar boy. While I cruised, I contemplated my good fortune; real life was surpassing my dreams.

As I parked and headed to my place, I discovered four Dallas cops, all squatting and bird-dogging my place. It looked like the party diehards migrated into my living room, and these boys in blue were poised for a bust. I playfully whispered, "What's up, guys," partly to alert them to my presence but also to hopefully deter them from taking down my crew. I succeeded, but not as intended.

I realized my misread of the situation a split second too late as a series of irrevocable dominos began to fall. Holy shit, did they come at me hard. Before I could wrap my mind around what was happening, they threw me into a fence and slapped on cuffs. One of the cops, a fat little squatty man, was quite pleased with himself. He seemed to relish the moment of catching a fish and watching it flounder . . . one of those mildly sadistic types. He enthusiastically stated that I was under arrest for public intoxication. Being shirtless and buffed, the nasty little turd asked what I did for work. I had a better-than-average chance that he worshipped the Cowboys and might let me go, so I told him I played in the NFL. It was like he caught the FBI's most wanted criminal as he joyously clapped his hands together, announcing, "Hot damn, boys, we got us a Cowboy."

Not my luck. I was fucked.

His partner pushed me toward the squad car as the little man had the gall to ask my position and what the other players were like off the field. Was Coach Landry a good guy? And on he went. I hoped this ad-lib press conference might get me released, but I wasn't that fortunate. Instead, they stuffed me into the back seat like I might fit if they pushed hard enough. I gave one last effort to prove my innocence as I blew fresh breath in their faces. That went over like shit in a punch bowl, so my night continued to spiral.

I was an oversized man in a clown car as my body contorted like origami and the cuffs cut off circulation to my hands. Then claustrophobia, which was my kryptonite since a young age, grabbed ahold of me as an unwanted old acquaintance. I had to find my Zen fast or risk more than just a public intoxication charge. I shut my mouth and focused on my breath.

After processing at the station, I joined forty sorry souls in the drunk tank for the next four hours. Pacing and contemplating, I reflected how this was my first, and would be my last, arrest. I didn't recognize it then, but the delicate dance between my darkness and light was seriously out of balance. These inseparable yet contradictory aspects of my being needed to be in harmony to bring my best self forward. And in the end, I wanted a future where I could look back with pride.

The arrest made a lot more sense after hearing about the rapid unraveling of the party only an hour before my ill-timed arrival. A village rent-a-cop, who tried to quiet the out-of-control revelry, was pushed into the pool by several drunk partygoers. Not just him, though. His gun, radio, and everything else got soaked. He was furious and ready for the big dogs to come in and handle the rambunctious crowd. His backup cleared the area, and all partiers who remained by the pool risked arrest. While I failed to get the memo in time, I got several hours of life-changing self-reflection and some sore wrists. Luckily, the Cowboys never got a whiff of this rookie outing, but I would never forget it.

Despite the mayhem, I wasn't quite ready to leave Greenville Avenue in the rearview mirror. How could I? It was home to the red-hot Café Dallas and a bevy of bars, nightclubs, and strip joints. It also had the number one pickup spot in all of Dallas, Tom Thumb Grocery Store. Surprised? Yeah, so was I. And guess where I did all my shopping? It wasn't uncommon to walk into the store and see many loaded carts abandoned for something fresher. Given the area's vibe, a seedy entrepreneur opened the Tub Club nearby. The concept was deceptively simple and appreciated for its novelty and proximity to the grocery store. I could rent a room with a hot tub by the hour that catered to newly acquainted couples with its red velvet walls and sticky sweet aroma. I felt dirty before I even entered the room. That was Dallas in the early 1980s, for better and sometimes worse.

The city's motto was work hard and play hard. The play part got plenty of attention with unlimited oil money flowing and the show *Dallas* gaining in popularity, setting the stage for an age of larger-than-life parties with loose morals. Meanwhile, south of the border, Pablo Escobar worked nonstop to funnel eighty tons of cocaine each month over the border and into party towns like Dallas. Not surprisingly, the accessible drug flowed freely, along with the entry of a relative newcomer to the party scene, Ecstasy, also known as MDMA. There were plenty of options throughout Dallas for anyone looking to up their party game or escape the pressures of life. While the scene was entertaining, keeping my internal compass calibrated became increasingly difficult.

Attempting to settle my angst in this unfamiliar city and over apartment life, I bought a house in north Dallas in a family-focused neighborhood. I loved the idea of having a home. Plus, it stood a mere fifteen minutes from the Cowboys' training facility, increasing my chances of arriving on time. The three master bedrooms provided a spacious crash pad for all my Iowa buddies who also migrated to

Dallas. They were the perfect antidote to football. They were fun, easy, and ready to rip up the town any night of the week. Remarkably, they all held their heads together during the day but let loose like the rest of Dallas once it hit five o'clock happy hour. I managed to temper the neighborhood's initial excitement about having a Dallas Cowboy in the community with my open-door policy, music, and backyard hot-tub antics.

Not long after moving in, I hosted a door-busting keg party with all the trimmings. My neighbor stopped by to introduce himself early the following day and invited me outside to meet his family before they left for church. In truth, he wanted to expose the collateral damage of plastic cups, beer cans, and tire tracks across multiple yards. The carnage was mortifying. I didn't want to be a crappy neighbor or fall into the selfish knucklehead football player stereotype. Bottom line, this was definitely not the way to embrace the new neighborhood.

As we walked, I noticed that my house shorts were nearly see-through. So, my junk was hanging free for all to see on a bright Sunday morning. None of my neighbors were thrilled with this encounter on their morning walk or drive to church. So much for enhancing the neighborhood. While I wasn't about to completely change my behavior at age twenty-three, I knew my careless ways would have to end eventually.

Living in this nice neighborhood meant a hefty mortgage, so I found a talent agency to help me make a few extra bucks in the offseason. I must've been desperate because I discovered a department store catalog years later that gave me a good laugh. I was standing in boxer shorts and matching knee-high socks with five neckties neatly draped over my arm as I looked into the distance. What was I thinking? Then I was plastered on the back of city buses mimicking Clark Kent, *ugh*. It was all worth it, though, because my mortgage got paid, and the parties raged on.

Earning Extra Cash

I also jumped at an opportunity to serve as the talent for a fateful NFL-themed Caribbean cruise. The plan was to join three other players to entertain over a thousand vacationers ready to talk football, wade in the piss pools, and cut loose at the ship's karaoke bar until dawn. I had no idea how many renditions of Kim Carnes's "Bette Davis Eyes" or Joan Jett & The Blackhearts' "I Love Rock 'n' Roll" awaited me. But I was always up for getting paid to schmooze, so I agreed without a second thought.

Upon boarding, I learned that the other three players canceled at the last minute. So, I would be the only NFL entertainment for the entire week. I practically fell over upon hearing the news, but my contact didn't break stride. She launched into the week's agenda with the litany of NFL talks and question-and-answer sessions before nightly dinners. Holy shit, I was going to earn this check. Sensing my disappointment, she supplemented her summary with what she thought was some kind of perk: I got to judge the karaoke contest every fricking night. Lucky me. I was ready to jump ship, but it was far too late to back out.

So, the liner set out to sea, and I took to the decks to meet my new friends for the week. As I meandered through the decks, I discovered my mug on every NFL poster throughout the colossal vessel. I was usually hidden on the offensive line, so I was amused by this rapid ascent to A-list status. It certainly helped that I'm a serial extrovert, so I dedicated the week to hamming it up, connecting with fans, and doing my best to represent the NFL well. "Hey Steve" became my call sign that someone wanted to chat or buy me a drink no matter the time of day. They didn't care if I was sitting with a group or had two margaritas in my hands, more drinks were coming my way than I could handle.

Well-oiled from eight hours of cocktails the first day, I grabbed the mic and did my football shtick. Yacking about some topic and answering endless questions, I didn't remember much, but I got some rave reviews. With a couple of vodkas for dinner and a side of meat, I kept my table entertained and then dragged them all into a karaoke contest. After singing backup for everyone and downing drinks with each table, I finally crowned the winner and stumbled off, trying to find my room for the next half hour.

My quarters were actually a glove compartment with paper-thin walls. So, I got to fall asleep listening to the couples on both sides banging away—lucky me. I was counting the minutes by the end of the first night and couldn't wait to get home. After a couple more days of mind-numbingly predictable patterns, a few crew members took pity on me and brought me to the rear bowels of the ship to hang with the crew. This became my safe place at night because they weren't there to party. My remaining time was divided among the crew taking me to secret destinations at port, doing my nightly talks, dinner, and karaoke. Then I would hide out with the crew and fantasize about what I'd do with the money earned on this floating fun house.

Like many other professional athletes with a decent flow into my bank account and dreams of a long career, I bought a flashy new Cadillac Biarritz convertible right off the showroom floor. It was an eye-catching Cowboy blue with a white top and spoke wheels. The scene was ripped from an old car commercial as I strolled into the dealership sporting my Afro, gold chain, and half-buttoned shirt. I pointed to the flashiest car among them and watched as the staff mobilized to open the glass doors and roll out their centerpiece. The cash deal was done within fifteen minutes, and I drove off with one hot ride.

While it wasn't the most practical purchase, I loved cruising on hot Dallas nights, cranking tunes with a cold one in hand. Hey now, no judgment: it was legal to drink and drive in Dallas in the early eighties if you were under the DUI limit, which I was most of the time.

My car caught the attention of onlookers, but there was one admirer whose interest caught me by surprise. It was a hot summer day, and I was returning from Tom Thumb supermarket—where else? As I entered my garage, I noticed the shimmer of a car as it pulled in behind me. I looked back as the car door swung open and watched a slim ankle in a sky-high heel hit the driveway. I was intrigued. This tall, cat-like blond stepped out to greet me with a devilishly sexy smile that lit my fire. Nothing about her facial expression suggested that she was lost or searching for another house in the neighborhood.

As she introduced herself, it seemed like Cindy knew what she wanted, and it wasn't a friendship. The ring on her finger was no impediment, so I served as her side dish over the next couple of months. This worked for me since I had a girlfriend and wasn't looking for anything more. I watched other players struggle with the balance of a football career and family, so I vowed to wait until my playing days were behind me. Cindy's demands of my time increased as she dropped by my house more frequently. When she arrived one day with the gift of a stereo system, I realized that I needed to both literally and figuratively pull the plug. I drew the line at boy toy.

I'm convinced Cindy wouldn't have dug me if she had known what happened a few weeks before we met. A memory that still lingers, and resurfaces far too often at reunions, took place at a massive hotel hosting a busy nursing convention. I was there with the rest of my Cowboys' rookie class for pre-camp training. The second night, I met my teammates at the bar to replenish the day's fluid loss. Nothing seemed out of the ordinary . . . at least not yet. It was another sweltering summer night, so I donned a featherweight pair of white linen pants and a Hawaiian shirt. I remember thinking I looked pretty good as a few nurses joined us for drinks.

I caught a quick buzz and excused myself from the group. I headed across the busy lobby to the lavish bathroom, where I steadied myself up to a urinal. I sensed some gas coming and waited until everyone left the bathroom to handle my business. Feeling happy-go-lucky, I wanted to entertain myself with the loudest fart I could muster. But I miscalculated. It wasn't gas but horrendous diarrhea. It plastered the back of my pants and shot down my legs onto the floor. My favorite pants were soaked beyond recognition. I was mortified and peered over my shoulder to the opulent sink mirror. I now had thin brown and wet linen pants that stunk beyond belief. I waddled into a stall, followed by the next one, using up all the toilet paper available and cleaning the best I could while attempting to restrain my gag reflex.

I couldn't help but laugh as I spotted the small, scented candles surrounding the vanity. Nothing at my disposal could handle this predicament unless it involved industrial cleaning equipment. My last task was figuring out how on earth I would get up to my room unnoticed. It also dawned on me that I had left my wallet on the table with the cute nurses, but that was an impossible retrieval mission given the circumstances. Forget my wallet; I wasn't going back to that table now. . . . You couldn't drag me.

But how would I get through that crowded lobby? I could no longer stay in the bathroom because of the mess and the stink, so I braved the world with my ass clinging to the perimeter. I shuffled around the main lobby to the adjacent elevator, where I pushed the button with ferocity. I understood my predicament was bound to be discovered. . . . This situation was about to go from bad to worse.

The doors parted, and a flood of bodies exited, but just as many swelled into the tight space. I took a position against the side wall, closest to the exit but next to a hot nurse whom I had eyed at the bar earlier. As the doors slid shut, everyone started looking around, wondering why the elevator smelled like an outhouse, followed by a hunt for the culprit. The nurse surmised that it was emanating from me and inched away. . . . So much for that potential hookup. Since there would be no clean exit when we hit my floor, I decided to race out, not look back at any cost, and scurry to my room in shame. I tossed my pants and collected my wallet a few hours later while making sure not to run into the hot nurse. Later, I learned that many other rooks contracted a bug from the water we consumed at practice that afternoon. But none of them could match my story.

Meanwhile, on the field, I managed through my own set of challenges. My relentless offensive line coach, Jim Myers, zeroed in on me like an attack dog. No matter what I did, it wasn't good enough for this perpetually irritable guy. He barked and carried on about pushing harder, getting into a lower stance, not taking my eyes off my opponent's chest . . . and the list went on. Years later, he explained that his approach was to figuratively "put a whip" to a player to see how he reacted. This would determine if they were a mule or racehorse. Once I outgrew my rookie status, he referred to me as a racehorse. I guess this was supposed to erase the emotional mindfuck I endured under his tutelage. But if pressed to admit it, Coach made me a better player. In addition to being on all the special teams, like most rookies, I also got my fair share of playing time in the third and fourth quarters, partly because of our team's dominance but also because I never gave up, just like a good racehorse. I would stand at the ready, close to the coaches, and never sat down in hopes of getting some action.

My eagerness paid off in spades one Sunday in Dallas. It was fourth down as the punt team took the field. Punters always count the guys protecting them, and there better be ten joining him on the field. After a quick count, he waved his arms in panic. They needed one more blocker. I looked around, but no one scrambled to get out there. So, I bolted onto the field and into the empty spot to prevent an unnecessary time-out. My peacock feathers spread high and wide as I strutted back to the bench with a host of slaps and "attaboys" shouted in my direction. This quick thinking and lack of hesitation earned me a spot on the punt team from then on.

The incessantly pacing, dirt-kicking Mike Ditka was my special teams coach and a great mentor. Getting a wink and fist pump from Iron Mike for a job well done was rare and an honor akin to throwing red meat in my direction. Ninety percent of the time, he was in someone's face, chewing them out, and giving an icy *I'd kill you if it was legal* glance that crushed most players. However, I was lucky to be on the receiving end of the tame ten percent that he rarely displayed in public.

Ditka took me on walks several times during my first year to impart his wisdom when he sensed my frustration mounting. He reminded me that everyone on the field possessed the physical tools, but what would separate me from other players was found from the shoulders up. Since then, I've passed that wisdom on to many since it applies to all, regardless of their sport. As only Ditka could say, while pointing his sausage finger in my direction, "You will get beat and get your ass kicked. Be a quick study and learn how to adjust on the fly. And no matter what, never make excuses." Much wisdom was packed into his comments, and it was put to good use over the next eleven years of my professional career. Then Ditka paused, spit, and summed it up with straight talk: "Bring your lunch box for a long fight and remember that you're only as good as your last play. Don't ever forget that."

Lucky for me, one of my last plays with the Cowboys was one for the books. It took place in the Minneapolis Metrodome, my hometown, in full view of my parents, buddies, and neighbors. The day started off with some disappointment about the thirty-five terrible seats I secured for my crew. They were positioned in the end zone between the goalposts and three rows up. Not ideal, except for this game. Given what was about to transpire, it turned out that their seats were some of the best in the house.... That was just my good fortune.

I started the second half with the kickoff return team, but our returner fumbled the ball. We recovered on the goal line, the worst possible starting position. As I trotted off the field, the offense came on showing their disappointment in our execution.

Just as I hit the sideline, Coach Myers, with his bloodshot eyes and a wad of gum protruding from his lower lip, barked for me to fill the right guard position. Meanwhile, the regular starter fiddled with his shoe, trying to shove it back on with no luck.

"Me, Coach?" I shouted, still out of breath from the last play as I attempted to absorb this turn of events.

"Yeah, Wright, go!" Coach yelled, chomping away and widening his eyes to instill a sense of urgency.

I was going in at a critical time, with the intensity redlining and our backs against the wall on Monday Night Football. These night games were my religion since I fell out of my highchair. Now I ran headlong into a childhood dream as I scrambled back onto the field. Thank God there was a well-timed commercial break to give me a chance to absorb the scene.

My new vantage point was priceless. It was an out-of-body experience standing in the huddle with guys like Drew Pearson, who, five years earlier, caught a fifty-yard touchdown pass, coined the Hail Mary, to beat the Minnesota Vikings during the playoffs. I remembered the game like it was yesterday. I was in tenth grade at the time, freezing in the stands, and now we were slapping five in the huddle. Holy shit, I was one lucky guy. And standing across from me was Tony Dorsett, whom everyone idolized. He was one of the best running backs in the NFL and my fricking teammate.

I took it all in as the youngest member of the huddle. Meanwhile, the veterans stayed loose and chatted like it was just another day at the office. Beyond discussing game tactics, they mentioned their relief to play indoors on this frigid January night in Minneapolis. These Dallas boys weren't fans of the cold, and I couldn't blame them. I took a minute to scan for my family and friends. I found them, eyes glued to us, and I flashed a thumbs-up with my insides screaming, *Can you believe my fricking luck?* It was the greatest body-wide flood of goosebumps that I had ever experienced.

Our quarterback, Danny White, organized us in the back of the end zone and called the play. As I took my position, the pressure mounted to execute my new assignment flawlessly against my All-Pro opponent, Doug Martin. I was in the big time, with my teammates depending on the other four linemen and me to help get us out of this hole. The play was called for Tony Dorsett to run straight up the gut to secure us some breathing room.

At the snap of the ball, I came off the line with so much pent-up energy that I exploded into Doug like a grenade. To my surprise, I managed to wall him off as Tony's feet flew by me. I clambered to get up, but he was long gone, through the middle and cutting right up the sideline for ninety-nine and a half yards: the longest run in NFL history.

We all danced in the end zone and trotted off the field after what would be my only offensive play of the game. How lucky was I? Tony's shoes, the ball, and video coverage went directly into the Hall of Fame in Canton, Ohio. I was so glad my family and friends had an enviable vantage point to watch this record-breaking play develop. The starter got his shoe back on and retook his right guard position, and my one play landed in the Hall of Fame. I'll take that trade any day.

While some games left me high on life, others turned into football lows. One such horror occurred when I was forty seconds away from the Super Bowl. We were in the lead the entire game, with my fellow rookie, Everson Walls, picking off two of Joe Montana's passes. Meanwhile, Ronnie Lott was flagged twice for rough play. San Francisco was practically giving us the game.

Danny Spradlin and I were already celebrating in anticipation of our trip to the Super Bowl. The closing minutes brought out desperation as Joe Montana slung a hope and a prayer to Dwight Clark. Everything entered slow motion as Dwight sprung for an amazing touchdown forever labeled The Catch. It was a collective slap to our faces as their prayers were answered. Candlestick Park exploded with elation as fans poured onto the field. The volume of people overtaking the area grew exponentially, and security panicked. We were told to bolt for the locker room door as fast as possible, but it was an obstacle course of humanity. The safety hatch seemed miles away. I started to freak out as I was grabbed from all sides. Then my survival instincts kicked in like never before. Anyone between me and the locker room door was roadkill. I was agnostic to age, gender, friend, or foe as I ran over everything in my path as if my life depended on it. Other players flooded into the locker room in shock, minus a helmet, jersey, or shoe, but we all made it to tell the tale of the almost Super Bowl of 1982.

Beyond those painful moments on the field, I observed some pain-filled minds in the locker room. Few players were as volatile as one defensive end I practiced against daily. He was 6 feet, 7 inches tall, 260 pounds, and ripped with about 5 percent body fat. While he was strong as Hulk in the weight room, he was a walking time bomb full of C-4 and ready to explode on or off the field. I believe steroids played a major role in his volatility since they were still legal in the early 1980s. We had plenty of slugfests after the whistle, during practices, but we always left it on the field.

I enjoyed this teammate but knew to steer clear when he was in a mood. One night, a group of us were watching TV when he came in after a couple of hours with his girlfriend, mumbling a host of obscenities. We sensed the fuse was lit, so we kept our heads low with all eyes on the TV to avoid provocation. I managed to sneak in a side-eye to one of my teammates on the adjacent couch, who responded with a nearly indetectable head nod acknowledging the chaotic energy that just entered our lighthearted sanctuary.

Our enraged teammate stomped by us, not even attempting human posture, and punched a five-foot-tall standing lamp into the wall, bulbs popping as his follow-through left only the base and the stem visible. Then, without skipping a beat, he ripped it out, tossed it like trash, and barged into the other room. He slammed the door so hard that it barely hung on for the rest of training camp. We just sat there, watching our show like we had seen this storm before. I'm unsure what the maids said about it the following day, but we had a new lamp and patch on the wall by the afternoon.

Even outside of the world of football, his behavior was erratic. One night, he got into a dispute over a parking spot at a Dallas nightclub. He approached the tan sedan with a hard, steady rap on the window to address the injustice of taking his parking place. The tinted window slid down, and a gun jutted out, blowing a hole through his stomach and untucking his shirt on its exit out his back. As the car bolted from the scene, he staggered around the parking lot until he dropped. Much to the amazement of all who knew about the incident, he was back on the field within five months of surgery and rehabilitation. He was crazy tough, all gas and no brake, but far too unpredictable off the gridiron.

It's impossible to discuss football in the early days without addressing steroids that the NFL didn't ban until 1983. When I arrived in 1981, I swore to avoid them. However, the pressure to be bigger was intense since size, strength, and speed offered decisive advantages. This was also when the Washington Redskins introduced their behemoth 300-pound offensive linemen, "The Hogs," who employed a smashmouth bulldozer mentality across the line. It was clear where the game was heading, and with the Cowboys averaging just 275 pounds on the line, they wouldn't be far behind the trend.

I managed to sniff out steroids from a teammate during my first offseason and began the unpleasant task of jabbing an enormous needle into my butt cheek. I also added Dianabol and was amazed at how quickly I gained fifteen pounds of muscle and maintained a pleasant amount of roid rage to get through the early part of my second season. I held onto much of the gains by choking down a small pasture of cows and obsessively pounding weights. But the league banned all anabolic steroids the following year. While plenty of guys continued, the risk of testing positive was too consequential. My common sense prevailed. I stopped cold turkey and didn't look back; today, my body thanks me.

While many players were remarkable, the Cowboys cheerleaders were mesmerizing. It was weapons-grade recruiting material to include their annual calendar in the package sent to attract football standouts. I coveted that flashy, eye-popping calendar. The cheerleaders were all gorgeous, my type in every way: athletic, good-natured, and smoking hot. When I joined the team, though, the front office enforced a clear dividing line between players and cheerleaders. We even operated out of different buildings to avoid muddying the waters. This was business, and we all needed a daily physical barrier as a blatant reminder . . . more for the guys than the girls.

I planned to respect this division because I didn't need to give the coaches any excuse to chew me out. But, even with the best intentions, things happen. Like the rest of Dallas, I was out at the bars with my roommates mid-season, enjoying an extended happy hour. I scanned the crowd for some amusement when my eyes zeroed in on a stunner at a table beyond the bar. I knew her face from somewhere, but I couldn't place it. My crew continued to put back the bevy of drinks at our disposal with the occasional free round because having a Cowboy or two in the bar was good for business. As the evening wore on, I was getting drunk and fearless. I was staring at her as I studied the wall calendar in college. We caught eyes, and it clicked. She was one of the veteran Cowboys cheerleaders, Sarah, a stacked, brunette knockout who got her own page in the calendar, plenty of time on camera, and loads of respect from the organization for the attention she brought to the franchise.

Once Sarah caught me staring, she shot a flirty smile in return. . . . Game on. She angled her head toward the door, and without hesitation, I grabbed my keys and trailed her without even signing off with my crew. My guys didn't flinch, with one yelling as I headed for the door, "Go to her place; ours is a shitstorm."

I don't recall any conversation once we reached Sarah's apartment. If I'm completely honest, I only remember seeing her top come off and registering the pink wallpaper behind her silhouette. The next thing I knew, the morning sun was blinding my eyes, and I was wincing with a dull ache in my skull. I was severely hungover and still wearing my shoes. Meanwhile, Sarah was sound asleep, and I slipped out to avoid an awkward interaction. So much for that longtime fantasy. I guess some things are better left to the imagination.

After that experience, I began to appreciate the building separation between players and cheerleaders, and I'm sure Sarah was good with that too. I did whatever I could to avoid her and succeeded by some miracle. While she taught me a good lesson to keep my head on straight, my experiences with other women in Dallas continued to challenge my Midwest values. I learned a lot that year with Cindy the pursuer, and Sarah the professional, but my most eye-opening experience was because of my only real girlfriend in Dallas, Tina. As wild as I was, she pushed the limits for this traditionally minded kid.

About halfway through our relationship, Tina planned a night on the town, suggesting I was in for a real treat. I assumed this meant a great steak dinner, followed by a nightclub and a lazy morning without interruptions. It started innocently enough as we stopped by her friend's place. When we arrived, her girlfriend met me at the door half-dressed. I pretended not to notice as I turned toward some noise from upstairs. Then another girl came into view, scantily clothed, and all I could think was, great, these girls are going to slow us down. I reminded myself to be patient and just go with the flow.

As we walked into the living room, I noticed an overstuffed bag on the couch filled with colorful sex toys peeking out. Then a third girl entered the room, and my head nearly exploded as I put the puzzle together. I wasn't in Iowa anymore. This was Dallas, and I was about to get my Midwest mind blown. Nothing prepared me for this turn of events. But, staying true to my burgeoning life mantra, I would make the most of this opportunity too.

CHAPTER 2

BORN A BEAST

To say that I was a noticeable child might be an understatement. The family joke was that when walking through a doorway, I always hit my head on both sides of the frame, catching everyone's attention. Maybe I was a bit uncoordinated, but I had an unusually large noggin' that was an early indicator of my future size. Born ten pounds and four ounces, I was basically a Great Dane puppy with a head and paws that didn't fit my little body. It was only when I hit 6 feet, 6 inches tall and 300 pounds that it finally made sense.

Me and My Head, 1961

Being a unique kid extended beyond my appearance to some of my early behavior. My propensity for the physical was first noticed during my brief stint on the show *Romper Room* at age five. As the biggest tot on the program, I habitually picked up other kids, carrying them around like my oversized personal toy collection. I have no idea why I did this, but no one else enjoyed it as much as me. Whatever the reason, it resulted in a curt call to Mom, requesting that I be retrieved from the set immediately and asked never to return. This should've ended my television career, but it didn't. Down the line came a few cameos and then *Survivor*, which rightfully concluded my primetime appearances after thirty-one straight days of starving myself on camera.

Eventually, I moved on from picking up other kids to pushing them around on the ice rink, football field, and basketball court. In fact, I fouled out of every—yes, every—high school basketball game because I loved to use my body. I was no bully, but my naturally laid-back personality took a back seat to my alter ego when it came to sports. It still amazes me that my parents got a front-row seat to this frequent metamorphosis but never showed an ounce of embarrassment. They accepted it as long as I kept that side contained. When it spilled into other parts of my life, they offered a swift course correction.

Childhood Crew, Third from the Left Flexing

Along with ice hockey and basketball came years of playing football and track, with a heavy emphasis on the field part of the sport. I experienced a fair amount of success and was selected as an All-American in track and field. But I was never the biggest star, which didn't bother me one bit. Being the best wasn't an expectation from my family or one I placed on myself. Unlike many of today's kids, who are often forced to select a single sport, I was encouraged to play everything with an intentional focus on variety and fun.

I believe the exclusivity of one sport would've burned me out by the end of high school and likely ended any hopes of an athletic career. It saddens me to see youngsters extolled as sports prodigies, flown all over the states to play in incessant tournaments. I wasn't a phenom. Growing up, my tournament travel radius didn't exceed fifty miles, yet I still made it to the NFL for a lengthy professional career. I feel that staying positive and playing with passion can take a kid further than those tournaments.

It's rarely discussed, but it seems the organizers benefit the most from these tourneys and camps with their high prices to attend, the special jerseys, hotels, and transportation. It sounds like a nightmare. If a kid is any good, they will be discovered, even if they miss the cross-country peewee league tournament promised to launch them... bull. I encourage my friends to put away their wallets and let their kids play.

My first sport was hockey, as it often is with kids in Minnesota. It was so much fun to bang the puck around, all padded up and basically a marshmallow on skates. While the other parents were in the warming house, Mom was all bundled up, standing by the rink in the snowbank, always my biggest supporter. I was a lucky kid. But by eleventh grade, hockey began to pass me by. I was no defensive help for the frustrated goalie as our opponents skated circles around me.

Meanwhile, in basketball, I continued to behave like a hockey goon, once taking out my frustrations on an opponent with a swift elbow to his jaw. As the referee approached me to retrieve the ball, I looked away and gave it a slow roll down the court, getting tossed and bringing shame to my team. In the aftermath, I struggled to answer a question I asked myself for years to follow: *who did I want to be?* A loving talk with Dad taught me that being aggressive and kind aren't necessarily in opposition. In fact, they needed to coexist, and I had to realign my light to a pathway that made space for both. I wanted to become strong enough to be kind. This would take decades, but my journey began there.

Given my physicality, I was far better suited for full-contact football. This sport would be my ticket for the next twenty-five years. I loved the collisions, mental agility, team mentality, and, most importantly, how it planted me in the present. I didn't think about what was for dinner or daydream about parties. I remained fully in the now, receiving immediate feedback. Either I stopped my opponent, or I failed and hurt my team. In a world full of gray, it felt like football was black and white.

I would be remiss to suggest the sport was one of mutual admiration from the start. Early on, I learned a lesson that righted my course. In my first year playing the game at age ten, I single-handedly succeeded in running off a decent coach. It was late September, and I had trouble adjusting from summer freedom to the confines of school and structured sports. I longed for my liberation and subconsciously decided to stand up to my immediate oppressor. Coach blew his whistle to call us in for an end-of-practice meeting. As we circled up to hear his words of wisdom, I stood on my head, thereby challenging his authority. I even succeeded in securing another misfit to join my protest through inversion.

The coach took one look at us clowns and slammed down his clipboard. "That's it. I'm done with these jokers."

I watched him stomp off from my inverted view, only amusing me further. In the middle of my belly laugh, I was waylaid by the assistant coach, who dragged me to his car and over to Coach's house, followed by a harsh reprimand from Dad.

Wildcat Football, 1968

Beyond sports, I was one of the lucky ones that grew up with a solid Midwest family. It was the stereotype seen on TV. Dad was a likable salesman for the Continental Can Company, while Mom was the traditional homemaker as well as my consistent sports chauffeur. I had one older sister, Julie, who, like me, was kinetically inclined. Dave, my younger brother, didn't come along until much later, but I'll get to that relationship soon enough.

Dad supported everything I did but wasn't afraid to drop the hammer with a solid ass whipping when needed. Outside of the occasional reprimand, he was forever willing to play catch after work, take me fishing, or do anything else that reinforced our innately strong connection. He taught me commitment and displayed his by rarely missing a family dinner or any of my home football games. This extended to my university games, which often became full-fledged family reunions with my grandparents and uncle's family meeting for extended tailgates.

Throughout my NFL career, Dad wrote letters of encouragement that always seemed to arrive when I needed them most, lifting my spirits or reminding me of my capabilities. I found out years later that he also wrote to Coach Landry while I was a Cowboy. Even more surprising, Coach usually replied, which was remarkable given the ridiculous time commitments of the coaching world. It warmed my heart to know that Dad was forever in my corner, shining his light and coaxing the universe in my favor.

Like Dad, Mom was a source of unshakable support. To say that I could do nothing wrong in her eyes was putting it lightly. This was tested to an extreme degree on a trip to Palm Springs during my football career. I sat her down and shared that I was having a son from a weekend tryst. I recall the blood draining from her face, her eyes glazing over. She didn't want to admit that in one fell swoop, I dishonored her belief in marriage, family, traditional fatherhood, and just about everything else serving as her bedrock. She paused for a long while and, in classic Mom fashion, asked if we would be late for our dinner reservation.

My mom, Marcia, was the daughter of Marine Brigadier General Russell and Edith Jordahl. Born in Shanghai, China, while her father was assigned to the region, she was raised prim and proper with house hands managing all aspects of daily life. Accustomed to this good living, she blossomed into a raven-haired, six-foot-tall beauty queen. She had several suitors with nerves of steel attempting a play for the general's daughter. One of those daring souls was my dapper father, Jerry, a newly commissioned Marine officer in 1947. Marcia fell for his warm Midwest demeanor that starkly contrasted her childhood's cold, strict home. For reasons that remain unknown, Grandma Jordahl never displayed much affection toward her daughter. In keeping with this model, Marcia held her own family at an emotional and geographic distance. As a result, I have few memories of the Jordahl's, except for one poignant experience.

I visited my grandparents in San Diego with a few of my buddies during my sophomore year of college. We sought a warm weather getaway as a reprieve from another endlessly cold Iowa winter. I traded my car with a friend who lent us his custom van, our damp, dirty-sock stinking home for the next ten days. Roundtrip, we logged over fifty hours of driving, spanning 3,000 miles, with a bunch of drugs, ranging from pot to speed, and an overabundance of psychedelic mushrooms. It was a miracle that we remembered anything from that trip and made it back intact.

We swallowed a mouthful of magic mushrooms as we pulled away from Cedar Falls. But we barely made it out of town before we needed to drop by a parent's house who just happened to be throwing a big party. High as kites, we convinced ourselves that stepping out of the van would expose our mushroom festival. So, we literally barricaded ourselves like paranoid cult members.

Undeterred, my buddy's mom rapped on the van window, insisting we introduce ourselves to their guests. It was a stalemate; we remained entrenched, and she was bewildered by these strange friends of her son. As a compromise, we pushed her offspring out like a hostage release, but only for a brief sprint through the kitchen to pillage food. Warm barbeque in tow, we skidded out of the driveway and finally started the journey.

We made it to San Diego without an overdose, drug bust, or speeding ticket. But little did we know that the drama was about to commence. We were headed to my grandparents' house for dinner, so we cleaned up as best we could, hiding the drugs just in case they wanted to see the van. I can only imagine how frightful we looked: road-worn, Afro-sporting, unkept college punks rolling up on the general's front yard.

Just as my Converse tread hit the driveway, my pistol of a grandma bolted out the front door with an air of accusation piercing through her wire-rim glasses. "Where in the Sam hell have you been? You're late!"

It was about 6:20 p.m., meaning we were a mere twenty minutes behind schedule after traveling 1,500 miles. Sure, this was a Marine family, but come on. I remember wondering if this was a joke as she shot off a few more barbs in front of my buddies, waving her bony finger in my face. Absolutely shocked by this greeting after the lengthy journey, I narrowed my eyes, bit my lip, and calmly but forcefully told my buddies to retreat to the van. There was no way I would endure the poor treatment my mother experienced throughout her life. As my eyes scanned the doorway, I met the gaze of my stocky, barrel-chested grandpa. I could tell he had witnessed this display from her many times. He pushed past to envelop me in a tight bear hug, shaking hands with my motley crew who stood dumbfounded.

While there was no forgetting the greeting, I followed Grandpa's lead, deciding to replace the bad with good that night. As the moon rose, there was plenty of cigar smoke, whiskey, and laughter on the porch as Grandpa held court deep into the night. Sadly, that was the last time I saw that good old soul. And as for my grandma, I left her and that unhealthy anger when the visit concluded.

On the flip side, Dad's parents, Gramps and Gramma, were a mainstay in my life, and I'm forever grateful for their presence. Gramps was a character, always doing something fun like pulling the grandkids in a toboggan tied behind the car or enlisting my help herding cattle. Gramps also taught me how to drive well before the legal age. We would meander on dirt roads outside Grimes, Iowa, that were endlessly straight and empty except for the occasional herd of animals. A good chunk of this acreage would be passed down through the generations—both a blessing and a curse, as I learned much later in life when our family's interests diverged.

Gramps was the big cheese in their tiny Iowa town, but he worked to blend in. I often tagged along to his office, including the customary strolls through the canning factory to check on everyone, always asking if their families were healthy or in need. I admired how much he cared as he expressed genuine appreciation and compassion for each employee. He understood on a fundamental level that success depended on the team's well-being. It was one of my earliest observations of servant leadership, where the goal of a leader is to support, not rule by authority. Gramma, meanwhile, was the physical embodiment of love through feeding and nurturing the grandkids. She was warm and giving to everyone she touched. It wouldn't be too far a stretch to draw a Mrs. Claus analogy with her rosy cheeks and a mound of white hair.

I spent a few of my preteen summers at my grandparents' farm after seeing a brochure for a boy's reform home strategically placed on the kitchen table. Now, that got my attention as I ran through for a swig of milk. My deep suspicion was that my parents desperately needed a break from their little hellion. They felt that doing some hard labor around my grandparent's farm, along with some innocent country fun, would serve me better than a boy's home, which remained the backup plan. They were right. I loved everything: the barns, tractors, guns, picking weeds in the bean fields, and endless hugs, food, and treats from Gramma. Like most everything else in my life, I discovered joy in the simplest of tasks.

I wasn't the only kid on the farm. Several summers, my sister, Julie, joined me. Only two years my senior, she was soft-spoken and kind. She also served as my steadfast partner during frequent moves as Dad worked his way up the company ranks. Fortunately, she was a jock like me, but in other ways, my complete opposite: quiet and happy to stay out of the limelight. We remained close throughout our formative years, including our college days when I visited her at the University of La Crosse in Wisconsin to join my one and only Tough Man Contest in 1979.

Julie was the instigator behind my entrance into the competition since her boyfriend had won the previous year. I never attempted anything of the sort and didn't think it through before committing to what became a human circus. With $1,000 in prize money for the winner, I figured this would be a more legitimate path to financial freedom than snatching food from the cafeteria, clubbing turkeys (more on that saga later), or selling my blood to cover beer costs.

Sure, I was a well-conditioned, 230-pound college sophomore, and not short on confidence, but also not eager to fight anyone.

My three college roommates came along for some entertainment while I joined twenty-five fighters of wide-ranging skill levels. I can still recall the stench of that well-worn arena. It stunk of dirty gym shoes, stale beer, and cigarettes, last wiped down sometime in the prior decade. Meanwhile, the crowd overflowed with overalls and feed hats as they discussed grain hauls and kicked around pork prices with Old Milwaukee's in hand.

I fought a total of four times that weekend, once during the preliminaries and three more fights, working my way to the finals with three two-minute rounds of almost anything-goes brawling. We wore an exterior cup, head guard, and sixteen-ounce gloves, just like Mr. T in his early years. I planned to watch a few fights before my scheduled slot to get the hang of this human cockfight. But just as I settled into the holding area, the lights dimmed, and my name was the first one called: "Steve Wright. Come to the center ring." Within a second, I was shoved forward by a handler. I can only imagine the dread on my face as I scanned the larger-than-expected crowd, jogged down to the ring, and climbed through the ropes to meet my fate head-on.

Somehow, Julie got to my corner before the fight began. With tears in her eyes, she mouthed through the anticipatory commotion, "I'm so sorry." In a moment of sisterly compassion, she clearly regretted getting me into this situation. But I didn't need that confidence killer before the first swing. While scanning the bloodthirsty crowd of beer-drinking yahoos and the stable of big-bodied misfits, I couldn't gauge if I would crumble, survive, or thrive in the ring.

My opponent was a 280-pound country bumpkin who appeared to be a mild-natured, baby-faced softie at first glance. Like me, not inclined to fight. So why was he here? I tracked his eyes that fell on a young woman, only about fifty pounds lighter in more fitted overalls, beaming with pride. I had his number now; he was only in that ring to impress his girl. I could win this match.

After the first couple of punches, I confirmed this was a gimme and a reasonable introduction to the ring. With a bit of cockiness mixed with watching too much Muhammad Ali and his sweet Ali shuffle, I started dancing around while delivering left jabs to his defenseless face. This garnered collective boos from the 4,000 in attendance. The fight was called with a broken nose for him and a win for me. I was getting the hang of this, or so my ego led me to believe.

The winners went on to fight three more times on Saturday. Much to my surprise, my first matchup of the day went smoothly, knocking out a formidable fighter who, on appearances alone, should've ended my run. But my second fight of Saturday's trifecta was the toughest. This went the full three rounds, kicking my ass.

As Ali would suggest, I had to keep my gloves where I needed them, protecting my pretty face. After one exchange, my opponent stumbled a half-turn and gripped the rope with both hands. He peered into the crowd, half-dazed with his back vulnerable. I glanced at the referee, who motioned to mix it up. Since it was the early days of this contest, and the rules fit on one side of an index card, there was no penalty for clocking an opponent in the back of the head. So, I went for it to end the madness. Lucky for him, he never saw it coming, waking up a minute later on the mat. One more fight, and I was out of there.

The last thing between me and my prize money was either a vicious-looking opponent full of tattoos, muscles, and a big Fu Manchu mustache or a sloppy potato-shaped guy that I knew I could beat. The former was no farm boy and stood more like a resourceful street fighter. The dude had to be experienced in ass-kicking and looked better suited for collecting late payments for the Gambino family.

When my name was called for the next fight, I climbed into the ring, ready to dominate. Then they announced my opponent, and everything began to move in slow motion. I watched as the one fighter I hoped to dodge sauntered up to the ring, oozing confidence. He shot me a death stare, assessing my vulnerabilities mounting by the second. I was sure the universe was about to hand me a significant blow, or more accurately, a fistful of humble pie. Would the first aid kit be enough to handle the ensuing wreckage? Maybe there was a local animal doctor in the crowd?

On a quest for survival, I devised a self-defense maneuver coupled with a one-armed windmill. I have absolutely no idea where it came from. Certainly not from any fight that I scrutinized on television as a kid. I felt my fist connect with a thud on my third overhead windmill. Looking up from my waist-bend, I watched this monster falling backward on his heels, about to crash onto his back. Relief flooded over me. Much to my amazement, I knocked him out cold. It was no stretch to call this win a miracle as my shoulders finally dropped and released a weekend filled with fight or flight tension.

As I gathered my prize money, I looked around the dingy arena one last time. I would never again be in the ring. I could bet my life on it. But I left the experience knowing I would always be able to say, "Been there, done that, and no regrets." It was another important reminder of a belief beginning to take shape and guiding me for years: say yes because anything is possible.

Tri-State Area Tough Man Contest, 1979

Beyond getting me into the ring, Julie was a reminder of what kind of person I wanted to become. Her experience inspired me to fight more important issues. While in Wisconsin, she dated a classmate looking for a job. Naturally, she asked Dad to pull some strings to get him something at the canning factory. He was happy to help until he discovered the guy was Black. Dad was enraged. It was the first time that I witnessed any prejudice from my parents. It hurt me to see this from my blood, pushing Julie away until they recognized their mistake. After many long talks, they gradually made amends. They worked to accept that judging on skin color wouldn't be tolerated by anyone they cared about, including their children. Julie's principles and insistence on doing what was right were great guiding lights for me. Being a good person meant treating everyone with a baseline of respect regardless of race, creed, or anything else.

And then there was my brother, Dave, the family surprise. He was nine years my junior and, in every way, my opposite. Most of our differences resulted from radically divergent parenting during our early years. As the first-born son, I was put to work managing paper routes, caddying, building docks, and digging snow out of driveways. The worst job was shoveling in the unrelenting snow. Winter in Minneapolis meant driveways needed to be cleared, and since it wasn't called child labor back then, I had the privilege of helping the family and our neighbors. So, if the snow was falling at bedtime, I was in for a rude awakening at 4:30 a.m. Half asleep and bundled like a burrito, I ventured out into the bitter cold to moonlight at age eleven.

Meanwhile, Dave, the baby, had the luxury of sleeping while the snow removal truck managed one of my former jobs. From work to responsibilities at home, countless examples of differences added up to make two very dissimilar people despite sharing the same bloodline. Our relationship soured eventually, but I learned several valuable lessons through our later interactions.

There were many family moves during my early years, so we needed to stay tight as we navigated new friendships. After my birth in St. Louis, we moved to Minneapolis, Old Greenwich, back to Minneapolis, then to Chicago, and around Minneapolis three more times, all before I left for college. As a result, I got comfortable with change, learning early to adapt or risk becoming an outcast. My spirit animal is a golden retriever, so I never had much trouble finding a new pack to run with, but through it all, my best friend was and still is me.

I found my longest-running group of friends during the Wildcat football days of fourth grade in the suburbs of Minneapolis. The buddies dominated each sport as captains and leaders who made the necessary grades, hung with the cool girls, and protected each other. If you messed with one buddy, you dealt with all eleven of the tribe.

Yet I was dumbfounded a few years later when three of them robbed our family home while we were out of town. I expected my parents to throw down a swift and merciless call to the police, but they took a different tact. Dad confronted the buddies, handing down punishment in the form of hard labor around our yard. They had no choice but to accept the hand of justice. It was actually quite merciful given that it turned out to be a day of basic yard work, followed by a lunch to end the matter. Once Dad saw the remorse in their expressions, it was history. He demonstrated forgiveness before my eyes. To this day, those buddies tell the story with much admiration for Dad.

The buddies were also fond of night-long excursions into our very own demilitarized zone: the Wayzata Country Club golf course. It all started during middle school on weekend nights when we camped in our fort, plotted, schemed, and ran like wild animals until dawn. When it was unbearably hot, our mission revolved around the course's sprinklers that we obsessively locked in place to flood the lush green. Once it was saturated enough for us to slide, we would sprint and dive across perfectly trimmed, outrageously groomed, soaking wet turf. It was the closest I came to flying at a young age. We repeated the slide route nonstop until one of us caught sight of the groundskeeper's cart beelining for us under the moonlight. Cue the witch music from *The Wizard of Oz* that would play in my head as his cart bounced across the fairway at full speed. Next, a buddy on alert channeled a prairie dog by sounding a chirping alarm. We scattered in every direction and met at the fort skidding in, out of breath and ready to do it again.

No matter how many times we pulled this trick, the night groundskeeper was forever one step behind. These all-night interval sprint sessions were so frequent that my running abilities improved tremendously that summer. I was one of the bigger guys and slower than the others, so I had to push extra hard. While this was critical on the green, the stakes were even higher at the shopping center. Donning an underwear facemask, and peering through a leg hole, we streaked through the mall on busy Saturdays for the sheer thrill of it. Many years later, during my professional football career, I found myself running with the faster-moving positions during practice, learning to keep up long ago.

Along with running, I started lifting weights during my first year of high school. By my junior year, *Rocky* debuted and lit the fuse to pound raw eggs, meat, and anything else I could consume to start packing on muscle. By my senior year, Arnold Schwarzenegger's *Pumping Iron* was released, and I was hooked for life . . . not kidding. My passion for weightlifting is as great today as fifty years ago, as strange as that may sound.

Summer Break with the Buddies

Along with working out like it was our job, the buddies found all sorts of things to stay entertained. During spring break of our senior year, we congregated in Fort Lauderdale for a change of scenery. While many flew down, my buddy and I took a forty-eight-hour Greyhound bus ride to Naples, Florida, and then hitchhiked across I-75, a.k.a. Alligator Alley, to connect with the crew. Thumbing rides in the late 1970s was commonplace, and we thought we had hit the jackpot when a customized orange hippie van pulled over to give us a lift. As we ran up to jump in, they slid the door open, and I stumbled back. It looked like it was on fire with pot smoke pouring out and hitting me with the force of a midsummer heat wave. In under ten minutes in the van's rear, we were ridiculously high with at least two hours of road ahead of us.

About an hour into the journey, we were shaken out of our haze by the sound of tires hitting dirt roads as the van pulled off the highway and down to the dark swamp. It had horror movie written all over it, from the moonless sky to the creaking van, as it navigated virgin, off-road terrain. I started to sweat and looked over at my buddy, who closed his eyes . . . was he praying? The driver slowed to a stop, fumbling in the glove box before sliding out. *Oh, man, this is it?* I wondered if a preemptive shout would be of any use. My buddy opened his eyes, tapping my leg to indicate that we should run for it, just like our golf course getaways. I shook my head, recognizing that in the dark, there was no way that we would find our way through the swamps unscathed.

Was reefer paranoia setting in? Most certainly. Then the driver, who was now in front of the van and illuminated by the headlights, started urinating all over the windshield. Everyone but us found it amusing, but at least our fight-or-flight response was back in check. I looked out into the night sky, whispering a word of gratitude to the universe.

The Buddies, 1978

Besides the plentiful golf courses that lined the Minneapolis suburbs, the buddies also spent a lot of time on Lake Minnetonka. We waterskied until dusk, always stopping at Lord Fletcher's lakeside bar for beers and burgers as the light descended and the girls came out. Sundays were the best day of the week at Lord Fletcher's, with plenty of boating action, music, and fun. A big storm moved in one Sunday evening, dumping overwhelming rain and lightning as we stomached the last of our burgers and downed our final beers. I had the good sense not to boat back home in these conditions, so I thumbed a ride home, expecting that Dad and I would retrieve the boat the following day.

The significant flaw in my plan was the lack of time to clean up the boat, meaning extracting the littering of beer cans and joints throughout the cabin. My parents weren't naïve and knew I had a beer or two, but nothing near the number of empty cans and reefers floating in the six inches of water christening their new boat. I was crushed, but Dad kept his cool, instead praising my focus on getting home safely. My parents always preached common sense and doing the right thing no matter the outside pressures. In this instance and so many others throughout my life, their wise words stopped me from crossing over the line.

CHAPTER 3:

TESTING GROUND

How did I end up at the University of Northern Iowa (UNI), originally a teacher's college? Well, I didn't think critically in those days. The free ride and second indoor dome stadium in the country sealed the deal. While I wasn't a high performer in the UNI classroom, I ended up in their hall of fame, managing to stand out in one regard.

College Days

Since I was unabashedly an athlete and a mediocre student at best, I have much more to share about football and university life than tales of my scholarly achievements. In fact, I didn't earn my degree because I signed a contract to play in the NFL rather than staying for a fifth year to complete my last few credits. I never regretted moving on, though. Things were happening fast, and I chose not to miss it. Once I left UNI, any thoughts of returning evaporated as the path in front of me was wild beyond my imagination. Nonetheless, I have plenty of memories from my university days that seemed outrageous at the time but paled in comparison to what came next.

Coming from an upper-middle-class Minneapolis suburb, I didn't anticipate the 180-degree change when I landed in Cedar Falls, Iowa. Along with the culture shock that comes from being surrounded by farms instead of cul-de-sacs, I went from a solid support infrastructure to none at all. Sure, I was ready to be out of the nest like most college freshmen, but my parents seemed equally prepared for me to find my way. They had done their job, and I needed some independent life lessons to shape me.

The university seemed to mirror my parent's approach. Unlike my future NFL teammates from Auburn, USC, and other fine schools, there were no posh dorms or special tutors for athletes. In fact, not a single professor even knew I played football. They didn't ask, and I tried to keep a low profile, weaving my way through marketing and business classes.

After sharing a single-sized room with two other guys in a triple-stacked bunk my freshman year, I was more than ready to move off campus. So, I joined three other buddies in a house to live free like adults. I was pumped about the arrangements until I drew one of the short straws, ending up in the dank basement for the year. Not wanting to throw my weight around with my new roomies, I begrudgingly moved all my belongings into the windowless hole, which consisted of a bed, flashlight, and space heater.

The basement was unfinished—more like never started—and had an exposed ceiling of pipes and twisted wiring that screamed fire hazard. On top of that, the cement floor and walls did a fantastic job of holding in the bitter cold during those long Iowa winters. Four months of the year, it was so frigid in that ice locker that my heater served as my best friend.

The other Frankenstein relegated to the basement had a tough time with the conditions, too. But he had bigger problems. His crazy stomach issues caused him to throw up three nights a week... and that was on a good week. Unfortunately, the thin sheet separating our basement rooms did nothing to shield me from the pattern of dry heaves that offered an unwelcome and highly consistent alarm throughout the year.

Not surprisingly, I jumped at any excuse to get out of town on the weekends, so when one of my teammates invited me to his family's farm for the weekend, I didn't hesitate. It couldn't be worse than my basement living, or so I thought. Most of my college teammates came from small hardworking and hard living communities that barely survived in the farming industry. When I pulled into his family's farm, I was shocked to see the conditions of the house. It weathered a few too many tornados, with most of the paint peeled off and the surrounding grounds in total shambles.

After he showed me around the property, including a barn full of cows and a massive pigpen, it was time to meet the family over dinner. Sitting down with his five brothers and sisters, his soft-spoken mother covered the table with more food than I'd ever seen in one sitting. It was pure heaven. There was no beer or wine, but instead mason jars of farm-fresh milk to wash down the chicken, pork chops, greens, corn on the cob, and potatoes three ways. Stuffed and beyond content, we moved to the TV room.

As I entered, I registered the smell of the earth with scents of moss. Looking down from the TV screen, I noticed the floor. It was all dirt with an area rug covering much of the space. Worried that they would look to me for a reaction, I did my best to flood them with compliments about the meal and their hospitality. They were great people, and I had a new appreciation for the term "salt of the earth," as they handled a difficult plight with grace. I also now understood why my teammate's attire rarely changed back on campus and his shoes were always in tatters. I was seeing poverty up close and personal for the first time in my life. It moved my empathy and compassion needle like never before.

When I did stick around campus, my roommates and I made our own fun. We performed monthly extractions from the school's cafeteria for a cheap thrill and to offset our mounting beer costs. The capers involved pulling into the loading ramp and sneaking into the rear of the kitchen after the cafeteria closed and the staff was upfront wiping down tables.

We came in with a few questions prepared in case we were spotted, but our records were clean, and there was never a hiccup during our heists. First, we would slip into the walk-in refrigerator, confiscating a box of ten dozen eggs. Then we grabbed two five-gallon milk containers and snatched a dozen pies from the rack. We were back in the car, pulling away in under a minute every time. Besides the adrenaline rush, the bounty of food was pure heaven. There was nothing like coming home from the bars and having a ten-egg omelet followed by a pie all to yourself. Not once did I consider that my scholarship could be pulled if I was caught. What's that line about not thinking beyond the end of your nose? Yup, I was as guilty as the buddies back in middle school who robbed my house.

Another one of our starving student favorites was the Turkey Grab-N-Go. Four of us loaded up a car around 10 p.m. and drove out to the turkey farms on the edge of town. But before leaving, we had to be stone-cold sober and fully stretched out. This expedition was like SEAL team stuff to us, but we lacked their brains and planning abilities for flawless execution. Yet success, however ugly, was paramount. We were four calorie-torching, perpetually hungry college kids in need of sustenance.

Our game plan was tight, or so we thought. We parked on the other side of the cornfield, leaving the trunk open, and covering it in plastic like we saw mobsters do in the movies. After a silent jog down the cornrow to the electric wire fence surrounding the barn, one of us raised a closed fist high to stop our movement in unison. It was critical to maneuver our bodies through the wires quietly, even if it meant stifling a yelp because any sound would wake the inbred farm dogs that would raise the alarm. Once inside the property, we gently cracked the massive barn door to expose no less than 50,000 fat turkeys milling about and softly gobbling with a gargled coo.

I was unfamiliar with the protocols on my first caper, bringing a billy club, which turned out to be a bad choice. Once we each had a bird in our crosshairs, one of us would give the visual countdown, and we all lunged at our prey. I swung my club as hard as possible, missing the turkey's head but breaking its neck. My eyes popped as I watched it take off running, dragging its head along the ground like a rickety cart with a bad wheel. Coming from Minneapolis, I had never witnessed this kind of crazy-ass farm shit, so I stood there dumbstruck. Thankfully, one of the experienced crew members pushed me to act as my wounded dinner carried on through the birdhouse, disturbing the peace. It was time to grab it and complete our extraction. With our birds firmly in our grasp, we bolted out the barn door as we heard the wild barks of deranged dogs coming our way. Without any doubt, there was a farmer scrambling for his pants and shotgun.

Our next obstacle was traversing the wire fence, much harder on the return leg given the plump birds in our arms. I had no idea how heavy and awkward these turkeys could be as I took my licks from the electric fence. Now, with an ever so slightly burning sensation in my arms, I completed the last leg. I reached the trunk, tossing the birds and making tracks with the lights off. For the next couple of hours, we cleaned those birds and lived as kings for weeks.

The birds weren't the only thing that risked taking a beating during my college years. My craziest memory belongs to a Friday night blowout party at my off-campus house. There were kegs of beer in every room of the well-worn pad. At peak capacity and deep into the night, a scuffle ensued between our wide receiver, Kenny, and another partygoer. One of my roommates pushed the scuffle outside, but as punches began to fly, he got in the middle and broke up the fight. Kenny swore revenge.

I heard about the fight but not the revenge part. I didn't think much of it as I was under the spell of a sorority pod, transfixed by an Iowa babe with a high blond ponytail and a distracting amount of baby-blue eye shadow. The party continued for another few hours and began thinning out around 1 a.m. Most of the party disappeared down to the bars, and I was nursing a good buzz when there was a sharp rap at my door that didn't sound like a fist, something more like a pipe. As I peered out the side window, I saw Kenny, along with a rather unhappy gaggle of brothers surrounding him. I cracked the door, sensing that something was awry, but then opened it further so as not to fire them up even more. Before I could get control of the situation, guys streamed into my kitchen, asking the whereabouts of my roommate. Half a dozen of these characters had rubber Halloween masks over their faces, carrying clubs on a quest for retribution. I kept reiterating that my roommate was at the bars, but this was met with suspicion. They wanted justice, and I was the only one home. I quickly surmised that I only had a couple of unsavory options: play possum, fake a heart attack, or punch the biggest guy in the face and run like hell. None of these would've saved my ass, so thankfully, I didn't listen to my inner voice for once.

But, with every passing second, my odds of coming out unharmed were looking less and less favorable. I still contemplated diving out the kitchen window to make a run for it, but another couple dozen guys positioned themselves right outside, anticipating an attempted getaway. Kenny's six-foot-ten-inch, mask-wearing, club-wielding, brutish sidekick was dying to hit something, so he unleashed a high overhead swing with his metal-capped club. It sliced through our cupboard and all the stacked plates like a wrecking ball, top to bottom. I swear I could've pissed myself, but Kenny pulled his attack dog back just then, yelling at everyone to clear out.

Kenny was the last one out and looked back, stating with conviction, "Tell him I'm going to find him." Luckily for everyone involved, Kenny never located my roommate that night. That was one scary moment, rattling me as my mind spun with questions: *Was the whole incident about race? Could I have done something to stop it?* It left me confused, feeling helplessly unable to fix it. It saddens me that Kenny and I never addressed the events of that night. Instead, as immature college kids sometimes do, we diverted our eyes when passing each other around campus and in the locker room. Neither of us possessed the emotional tools to work through that night with compassion and understanding. If I could rewind the clock, I would've grabbed lunch with Kenny and talked it out.

Over thirty years later, as the Black Lives Matter protests took hold, familiar feelings of angst emerged as I wondered how to make a difference. There is one thing that's given me comfort in the face of racism, on the football field and in the locker room. I've always experienced a racial utopia that I hope the rest of the world can achieve someday. In those spaces, there's no race, only brothers, and it's remarkable.

Beyond university life, football dominated my days. I was a decent player but nothing extraordinary. I played a little offensive tackle but mainly tight end during my sophomore and senior years. I missed the last four games of my senior season with a badly sprained ankle, which could have hurt my chances of being drafted, but everything turned out better than I hoped.

I remember the night of the 1981 draft like it was yesterday. There was a buzz in the air as I gathered with my crew to watch the events unfold, hoping for the remote chance of a late-round pick. It was improbable but not impossible, and my positive outlook and history of good fortune compelled me to wish for an outcome in my favor. As the hours ticked by, my chances faded fast, and my consumption of free-flowing beers from a nearby keg accelerated. By the time the draft concluded, I was foolishly drunk.

As luck would have it, three hours after the airing of the NFL draft, a weary, road-worn man showed up on my doorstep in Cedar Falls. What franchise was he representing? My mind spun through the teams that contacted me to show tepid interest. I prayed that he was with the Cowboys, and the universe delivered.

Cutting to the punch line with no added pizazz, the road warrior introduced himself. "My name is George, and I'm here to offer you a chance to sign with the Dallas Cowboys as a free agent." My eyes dilated as he leaned into me. He must have smelled the booze streaming from my pores and noticed the bevy of stains on my favorite Hawaiian shirt. Undeterred, he dictated orders to speed things along. "Get a drink of water, freshen up, and get in my car." He said it with such authority that I obliged. I took a minute to peer in the bathroom mirror, whispering to myself, "This is it."

George drove me to his hotel room and pulled out the contract, rattling through the terms. I did my best to appear contemplative. He rubbed his face in his hands, mumbling about his exhaustion and how I was his last signee after three consecutive weeks on the road. As my buzz mellowed and I regained my senses, I gathered the courage to push for a signing bonus. After another reflexive rub of his temples, George asked how much. I grabbed for a number aimlessly wandering through my head: "$1,500 to help me pack away some groceries."

"Groceries?" he balked. "$1,500 for groceries, huh?" I shook my head, momentarily out of comebacks. He broke from his weariness, ending the uncomfortable silence with a laugh. "Sure, kid, we can do that." New to negotiations of this magnitude, I could've asked for far more. But it was a flash of regret because I had just signed with the Dallas fricking Cowboys. I was on my way to the big time.

CHAPTER 4

GAME TIME

Many fans, even players, sometimes forget that the NFL is big business at its core. It just happens to be in the business of football—but about the bottom line and financial decisions first and foremost. I learned this the hard way as I was about to start my third season with the Cowboys. Hours before the fourth preseason game, I was abruptly traded to the Baltimore Colts, and it tore my heart out. I loved Dallas; I was settled into my home and playing for America's team. I was leaving all that to join one of the worst teams in the NFL.

It happened so fast that I could barely keep my emotions in check. We finished our pregame breakfast as Coach Landry methodically paced around my table. I was so young and green that I didn't pick up on any clues that would offer me the necessary time to prepare. When I finished my last bite, Coach leaned in right on cue. "Steve, take a walk with me." It was an order, not an ask.

One of my favorite teammates from those years was Butch Johnson, a flashy wide receiver who sat across from me at the breakfast table. He lowered his newspaper so I could see his eyes as he winced, and that was all it took for my heart to drop into a stomach full of eggs. On our short walk, Coach Landry explained that I was traded to the Baltimore Colts. My stomach cinched into a tight knot, and I could feel the eggs looking for an escape route. My vision narrowed, and my ears buzzed, so I only caught the tail end of his comments when he explained that they took the liberty of scheduling my flight to Baltimore at one o'clock. I would not return until the end of the season, five months later. This was just cruel; I was leaving that day without any time to get my affairs in order. At that moment, it was impossible for me to fully appreciate how frequently my life would pivot during the next ten years of professional football. But in those few minutes, I recognized for the first time that I was a product, not a person, when it came to the business of football.

My nascent negotiation skills earned me a few more hours of packing time before catching a four o'clock flight with everything I needed, minus my girlfriend and buddies, to make Baltimore home. On the flight, I shared my heartbreaking story with the attendants. They kept my cocktail glass full, offering a bag full of liquor bottles as I exited the plane. This was the only time in my life that I got drunk to numb my sorrows. Sucking down a couple more bottles on my taxi ride to the hotel, I stumbled in, with all my stuff in tow, as a shell of a man. I looked like merchandise that had fallen off the shelf.

My Cowboys days were over. I had a week to learn the Colts' offense before starting in Sunday's game. There was no choice but to let go of the past and fix myself firmly in the present. I wasn't going to risk another unexpected move. In time, I recognized that this trade served me well. The Colts could use my talents, and all the playing time fast-tracked my development. If I had stayed in Dallas, I could've remained a backup for the next year or two instead of diving straight into the Colts' starting lineup. Sometimes possibilities emerge in interesting disguises.

I made lemonade out of the Baltimore lemons and enjoyed the next year because of the strong brotherhood that developed. We fought hard and hung close despite enduring one of the worst coaches, Frank Kush, whom the NCAA canned in 1979 for grabbing the facemask of his punter. In fact, Coach's reputation was so poor that it contributed to John Elway's refusal to join the team. I had never witnessed so much bidirectional disrespect, especially after coming from the Cowboys' world-class organization just weeks prior.

Coach Kush entered the NFL with a small-man complex and an outsized chip on his shoulder in my eyes. He had no idea how to work with professionals, slinging insults in our direction. I distinctly recall his verbal dress down of a defensive lineman during a film review one afternoon. He appeared to question the player's manhood with insinuations about his sexual preferences, asking about the fun he had in the human pile-up. To add further insult, he pointed to his gait, suggesting he wasn't man enough. It was wrong and awful on so many levels. No one said anything, and I resisted the impulse to confront Coach until many years later when we had a few heated words. The guy still makes my blood boil.

The grand narrative of being manly was an outdated schtick that should have never persisted. But sadly, it was baked into the origins of football. The sport didn't rise to prominence because of ruffians in the streets, as many people romanticize. Quite the contrary. It was introduced into the Ivy League as a social engineering tool to harden boys.

Walter Camp, often described as the father of football, preached, "Better [to] make a boy an outdoor savage than an indoor weakling." These Ivy League bookworms were seen as too soft. And there was a growing fear that the next generation of leaders funneling out of top schools wouldn't be equipped to establish American dominance on the world stage. Those in areas of influence saw football as a substitute for war, teaching boys to absorb punishment and dish it out in return. Theodore Roosevelt reinforced this notion in his address at Harvard in 1907: "I have no sympathy whatever with the overwrought sentimentality which would keep a young man in cotton wool. Don't flinch, don't foul; hit the line hard!"

Along with the chest-beating macho stuff, I struggled to reconcile several head coaching selections when plenty of impressive position coaches stood at the ready. I shook my head when these experts, often coaches of color, were overlooked for jokers like Urban Meyer, who worked with college kids before joining the old boys club. Meyer, who

I felt was a drifting ex-college coach of questionable character with a shady past of cover-ups, was tapped before proven NFL coaches. Not surprisingly, Meyer, just like Kush and others before him, had no idea how to relate to professionals, nor professionals to him.

The league and its franchisees can do better in the selection of leaders. It sickened me that only five out of thirty-two teams had Black head coaches in 2022 while, as a race, they made up 70 percent of the players. Meanwhile, the league offered another song and dance about reform. The Rooney Rule, their weak attempt at a fix, requires teams to interview ethnic-minority candidates for head coaching and senior football operation roles. While many rebuff this example of affirmative action, I feel it doesn't go far enough to usher in long-overdue change.

With all these actions, it's no wonder that over a century later, the sport and its crowning achievement, the NFL, are challenged to right their course. Then you add guys like Kush and Meyer into the mix, along with a rebuff of diversity at leadership levels, and the hope for fundamental change fades fast. So, as a cog in a much larger wheel, I endured Kush just as other players tolerated Meyer. But this didn't stop my resentment from growing as Kush forced me on mandatory runs, regardless of injury status. Despite having a sprained ankle or a tweaked knee, I had to finish the course. After a year under this classless loser, I wanted out.

There were countless unsavory experiences with Kush, but one head shaker left me squarely in the wrong. I was nursing a grade-two ankle sprain before a game against the New York Jets in Shea Stadium during our 1984 season. The injury was bad enough to justify rest and rehab instead of standing on the sidelines. But once Kush learned of my plans to go to the city anyway to see my buddies, he demanded that I clock in at the stadium. His insistence wouldn't ruin my plans, though. Determined to let loose, I figured making it to the game would be a reasonable inconvenience on a Sunday afternoon. How hard would I party anyway? Famous last words.

It was a blast to reconnect with childhood buddies in their new haunts as they took on Wall Street by day and partied like fiends by night. Similar to me, they had work pressures and alter egos, but their replacements weren't waiting in anticipation of a statistically probable injury. Not to dismiss their stressors, especially on Wall Street, but professional sports have an ever-present angst of near-immediate substitution. It always left me feeling somewhat disposable.

But for that weekend, it was time to drop the worries and get to it. The moment my bag landed on the floor of their overcrowded apartment, I knew I was in for one hell of a weekend. It started with a few rounds of attitude adjusters, and then we headed out into the city lights. We piled into cabs like college kids on a budget because no one wanted to miss a joke, a pill of Ecstasy, or the passing of a flask.

We headed straight to Area, a hotspot in Manhattan that was new and, therefore, a place to be seen, with a line rivaling a stadium before a playoff game. It was the spot to rub shoulders with the likes of Madonna, Sting, John F. Kennedy Jr., Boy George, and Andy Warhol. While hot New York clubs came and went, we were lucky enough to catch Area at its best . . . if we could make it inside. Our cabby dumped us in front of the crazy line at the entrance, and the Ecstasy was in full effect. So, we had nothing but smiles, oblivious to the nearly insurmountable odds that lay ahead. Truth be told, we could've partied in the alleyway dumpsters and had a blast, given our altered state.

My only mild worry was not losing sight of the next day's game time of one o'clock. But after a few more pulls from the flask, I dropped that mental baggage along with the rest. It was party time. We were dressed to the nines with me at 290 pounds, yoked, and sporting a shocking electric-blue suit. As we took our place at the end of the winding line, I decided to boldly head toward the bouncers. I maneuvered through a few hundred people to shoot the shit with these guys who were better suited for the offensive line. Hoping I made an impression, I meandered back through the mass of humanity to my buddies shrugging my shoulders. Around midnight, the doors swung open. The head bouncer stood on his stool, pointing a finger in my direction. Great, challenge one of the night was behind us.

We were handed sunglasses upon entry, but sadly, I have little memory from the club, just a sweaty mess of bodies. I woke to find myself on my buddies' floor, busted sunglasses in hand, next to my bag where it all began. It felt like the prequel to *The Hangover* as I took bodily inventory. After validating that I still had feeling in all my fingers and toes, I turned to my other senses. I could hear my crew laughing and shouting at the TV from their couch position. Opening one eye to take them all in, I registered why there was so much animation in their voices: the Colts were beating the Jets. Cracking a smile, I peeled myself off the sticky floor. Then dread hit me with the weight of a brick. I wasn't on the sidelines and had no idea how to get there. Holy fuck, I was going to be in hot water with Kush.

After another few motionless minutes of processing my predicament, I pulled myself together and leaned against the couch. One of my buddies reflexively turned to hand me a beer but then paused as he took in my face. This was the first moment it dawned on him that I was supposed to be on the TV, not on his floor. But like a good buddy, he just busted out in laughter, shoving the beer into my palm. Sure, my wallet got a little lighter because of the fine, but it was worth it. I got to hang with my crew and avoid watching Mark Gastineau up close in his backyard.

The Colts ended the season in fourth place in the AFC East, at seven wins and nine losses, with just shy of an abysmal one-third occupancy average at home. That place was something else entirely, deemed "The World's Largest Outdoor Insane Asylum." My folks were accustomed to the highfalutin Texas Stadium and all the Cowboys luxuries, so nothing could've prepared them to sit with the last of the Colts' diehard fans when they came to visit.

As my folks and I split for the game, they went to their seats, and I headed to the locker room. They were all polished and ready to head straight to dinner after the game. But when I met them in the parking lot afterward, they were trashed. Mom's mascara and hair must have weathered a downpour, and Dad's comb-over spread like a sopping spiderweb. As it turns out, they were the target of a few full beers on the stadium stairs. Not surprisingly, they were one and done at Memorial Stadium. But they were happy to trek to Dallas anytime to watch me compete against my old team in style.

I loved playing the Cowboys on their home turf. I never held a grudge, but I wanted them to see what they gave away. While properly motivated, I still had to contend with the bonds that persisted with some old Cowboys teammates. One in particular, outside linebacker Jeff Rohrer, was a good buddy who was my responsibility one Sunday morning. We handled the battle as professionals: team first, friendship second. But midway through the game, a brawl broke out. Joining the fight was necessary, as neither of us could afford the laser pointing at us during Monday morning's film critique. We had to be seen punching each other and protecting our guys, justified or not. So, I grabbed Jeff, and we did it up for the cameras. It was an ad-libbed WWE wrestling match as we threw fake haymakers. Then we dropped to the ground, catching up on life while doing our best to appear like steamed elk with locked horns.

"Come out to the lot for a beer before you take off," Jeff grunted during our two-man melee. I nodded before the referees broke up the fight, and Jeff and I went back to work.

Just as I suspected, the fight was scrutinized during the film review session that Monday morning. As the coaches dissected the penalty and ensuing scrum, they circled a few guys who avoided the fight. Then the offensive line coach pointed me out, rolling around on the ground and punching Jeff.

"Look at Wright. That's how it's done," Coach said, pointing in my direction.

I just grinned and nodded. If they only knew.

While I prided myself on this performance-worthy display, there were several other standouts in my midst with the Colts. Offensive tackle Chris Hinton, first drafted by the Broncos and traded to the Colts as part of the John Elway swap of 1983, was a great addition to the roster. He was cool, smart . . . and draft-rich. It was a long-held tradition that high draft picks take some elder teammates out to a classy restaurant to celebrate joining the team. Instead of leaning on your new cubemates to discuss 401(k) options, we in the NFL liked to start off with a sizable hit to the wallet. Sure, it was nonsensical, but it generated new bonds and often a few good stories.

On that memorable night, Chris secured a table for our quarterback and ten linemen at the nicest establishment in downtown Baltimore. We were all dressed to the hilt, sporting suits and even a few combing their hair. While we walked in looking like overgrown choir boys, groomed and sober, that didn't last long.

Seduced by the façade, the maître d' made a fateful decision. He sat us as showpieces at a large table in the center of the opulent dining room. All the polished patrons enjoyed watching us for the first half hour. Parents would joyfully eye their kids approaching us for autographs and photos. It was a scene straight out of a Hallmark special. But, with our courtesy welcome cocktails empty, it was time to get the night started.

As was customary, we ordered a dozen bottles of Dom Pérignon without glasses. We wouldn't need additional vessels to polish off this good stuff. Instead, a bottle was placed in front of each player in lieu of a water glass. As our volume began to pick up and more bottles were ordered, I was still coherent enough to observe the crowd. Like a temperature gauge in a sauna, their concern steadily rose. I got such a kick out of watching parents throw an arm around their kids to shield them from these cageless animals.

We downed steaks and piles of lobster as we sat at a feeding trough, quickly emptying our bottles of Dom to wash down the good eats. After we blew through the restaurant's reserves of the best champagnes, I helped our fun-loving, six-foot-nine-inch-tall

Canadian tackle to the bathroom. He started swaying like a ship lost at sea as he charted a path through the fine china-topped dinner tables. By this point, the other patrons watched in horror as the manager and waiters endlessly circled our table in a feeble attempt to contain the mess. The staff did their best to speed us along, but shit was going south fast.

Our tanked Canadian emerged from the gold-trimmed restroom with barf plastered across his suit jacket and pants, stinking worse than a warm compost pile. In his stupor, he slipped on his puke, scrambling across the slippery bathroom floor to rise from the regurgitated feast. He wasn't overly concerned, though, thanks to the booze. Instead, with a single-minded focus, he stood on his chair like a thick flagpole and proceeded to belt out his national anthem, "O Canada." The combination of his antics, the mortified staff, and patrons scrambling for their coats and kids caused all the players to double over in laughter. The night more than exceeded our expectations as the group bonded, sharing the story with great amusement for many years to come. Our man, Chris, went on to be inducted into the Colts Ring of Honor with seven Pro Bowls. Meanwhile, our beloved Canadian headed back up north to complete a lengthy career with the British Columbia Lions.

It won't surprise you that most of Baltimore, and certainly those poor restaurant patrons, weren't upset when the season ended. Nor was I. Once the last game was played, I left my apartment, dropped off my car, and jumped on a plane for Dallas, not knowing that I would never step foot in Baltimore again. During the middle of spring in 1984, I was caught off guard, just like everyone else, when the Baltimore Colts moved to Indianapolis in the dead of night. It was a much-needed change of atmosphere from the tired Baltimore stadium to the spanking new Hoosier Dome. The new digs were packed for every home game. It was a brilliant move by the owner, Robert Irsay, to slip out of a town that didn't support nor care for him or the Colts franchise. Even though we had a poor first season in Indy (four wins, twelve losses), the city loved us, and the team was tight.

But the Colts were one of the lowest-paying franchises in the NFL, so I struggled to get a decent contract. During the height of my frustration, an emerging group, the United States Football League (USFL), came calling, mining NFL rosters with big offers as bait. It was an easy decision, jumping to the new league and joining the Oakland Invaders. By this point, I understood the business of professional football: take only what I need for a five-month stay as it isn't home and unlikely to become one. This was a job that I just happened to love, but I learned not to get too attached to any team or city.

I thoroughly enjoyed my one year in the USFL. Sure, the league and talent were a grade below, but it had many up-and-coming stars and former NFL powerhouses seeking better packages. It boasted talented studs like Reggie White, Herschel Walker, Jim Kelly, Sam Mills, and Anthony Carter. Steve Young signed a forty-million-dollar contract with the Los Angeles Express one year before I joined and managed to jump to the 49ers as the USFL folded. So, he, like many others, made out well to work this angle.

The coach of the Oakland Invaders, Charlie Sumner, was previously the defensive coordinator for the Los Angeles Raiders. He was an agreeable coach as long as you performed, but if not, he could get ugly in a heartbeat. He would be defined as a player's coach, meaning there was an undercurrent of mutual respect. He seemed to like me, along with our center, Jimmy Leonard. One afternoon, as the team gathered at the Oakland airport, we were informed that the flight was delayed for a couple of hours due to weather.

As my buddy Jimmy and I kicked around ways to kill time, Coach strolled through the tight collection of families and leaned into us, murmuring, "Follow me." We fell in line, slipping out the front door like overgrown ducklings. "Meet me at the Tap Bar," he said, jumping into his town car. This seemed unusual, but when Coach told me to meet him, that's what I did, no questions asked.

"You guys like martinis," he stated—as opposed to questioning—

while we took our seats at the dimly lit bar. By our fifth round, a few other players caught wind of our whereabouts and showed up to partake. It was a great time until one of the front office guys broke up the party with news for Charlie that the flight would be delayed an additional hour. This didn't sit well with tipsy Charlie, now affectionately referred to as Coach Chucky. He slapped his hand on the nicked-up bar rail and wiped his sweaty forehead with a wet napkin as he attempted to pull himself together. Drunk as a skunk, he led the charge out of the bar and back to the airport.

We slipped into our gate area without incident, followed by Coach Chucky, who stumbled in, mumbling, "Where's the fricking plane?" as he collapsed into an empty row of seats.

With that, the front office staffer smirked and asked, "What the hell did you do to him?"

"Who?" I answered, flashing a smile with the pleasant buzz still in full effect.

Coach Chucky let out a guttural snore that ripped through the room and got everyone snickering, including the gate attendants who watched the show with great amusement. With Coach now under control, the front office decided to leave us alone but gave one last playful stare in our direction. It was a lost cause.

To celebrate a bye weekend, Jimmy Leonard, Monty Bennett, and I hit the road in my lady-killer Cadillac convertible. Our destination was Reno, Nevada, for a weekend of fun. After a couple of hours of mountain driving, we pulled into a tavern with a few horses tied up along with two tired pickups out front. It felt like I was walking into Clint Eastwood's *High Plains Drifter* as seven legitimate cowboys eyed us on our way to the bar. The space was littered with old cans and tabletops stained with dark rings from unattended beers. We grabbed our drinks and secured a pool table. Halfway into our first game, I could feel the bad juju developing as a few guys at the bar started muttering nonsense in our direction.

These characters looked messy, with permanent imprints of

dirt along their foreheads that lay in stark contrast to my crew. We were wearing flip-flops, shorts, tank tops, and aloha shirts, along with sunglasses perched on our heads like overgrown beach boys. It would've been impossible to look more out of place. The loudmouth of the mountain cowboys was the littlest guy. He sauntered over, offering some indecipherable insults while perching on the pool table, feet dangling like a mini man. We quickly developed an offensive plan with nods and a couple of side-mouth murmurs. The three of us weighed more than the seven of those pencil-necked barflies. Even though we were paid to crush people daily, I wanted to leave that world on the turf.

We established our dominance fast, hoping to end the scuffle before it started. I swung the heavy end of my pool stick like a baseball bat, stopping shy of the little guy's face to ward him off. While the locals came to his aid, we grabbed more pool sticks to serve as attitude adjusters. On the cusp of pandemonium, a loud crack captured everyone's attention. The big, battle-worn bartender possessed the best club of all. He charged at the little guy, pushing him out the front door and yelling at the others to get lost. He knew the locals and said they were trouble. After a few beers on the house, Reno was our next stop.

Reno-Bound with Jimmy

With Monty and Jimmy

As the 1985 season ended, we lost the championship to the Baltimore Stars in the Giant's Stadium. This was the last game played in the USFL, as the league promptly folded, shutting down as quickly as it launched. Coach Chucky was welcomed back to the Raiders with open arms while my fate hung in the balance.

CHAPTER 5

GLORIFIED RENEGADES

As the team saying goes, "Once a Raider, always a Raider." When Coach headed back to Los Angeles, he brought Anthony Carter and me to try out for the NFL team known best for its toughness, lawlessness, and win-at-any-cost mentality. It was a lionized mix of absolute rebels. I was all in and didn't hesitate to boldly run through with a floodlight of optimism when the door to this mayhem opened.

I was welcomed into the no-rules Raiders but kept my head on a swivel with this bunch. True to their reputation, they were uncontrollable and unabashedly violent. I never knew if I would be part of a bench-clearing brawl or be the target of retribution because of a teammate's foul play. This was on top of the stress of spending three hours battling an opponent built like a grand piano. I would take on future Hall of Famers like Reggie White ("The Minister of Defense"), Kevin Greene, Bruce Smith, Super Bowl MVP Randy White, and other tough guys like Neil Smith and Brian Bosworth.

While Randy was a teammate in Dallas, he was a foe when I played for other teams. That's right, allegiances changed fast in the NFL. We became blood rivals in under a day. But he was never one to bond with too many anyway. That might've been because he was only there to bring pain, mashing anyone in his way. His nickname summed it up well: "The Manster," half man, half monster.

During our first game with opposing teams, I played right tackle over the Manster and Ed "Too Tall" Jones. I was in for a long day at the office with these two tough guys. It would've been wise for me to get my job done with no extra chatter. No need to awaken the Kraken. But despite that wisdom, I couldn't help myself and instead pressed my luck.

You know when a baseball player hits a home run, it seems effortless because they connect with the sweet spot on the bat, jacking the ball into the upper deck? Well, I caught Randy in the sweet spot of his chest coming off a stunt. With remarkably little effort, I launched him onto his back. It surprised the shit out of me because nothing was ever that easy. It was one of the better and more memorable hits of my young career. And I just couldn't leave it at that. I pointed down at him, and we exchanged a couple of expletives. Then I ran off in pursuit of hitting someone else without giving the interchange another thought.

Paybacks come in many forms during a game. Mine was delivered two quarters later. We were kicking an extra point, nothing particularly noteworthy. All the linemen turned our bodies sideways, placing our heads on the man inside to establish an unbreakable wall. It was great protection for the kicker but created a target-rich environment for an easy assault on the linemen. At the snap of the ball, Randy didn't even pretend to do his job. Instead, he stood and punted every ounce of air out of my body. I dropped, gasping for air. How a referee missed this violent act boggled my mind. All I got were the nostrils of the official staring down, half-concerned, asking, "You ok?" Meanwhile, Randy wagged a finger, offering his signature deranged, shit-eating grin. There wasn't an ounce of compassion or empathy coming from this beast, but I should've expected it.

I believed in conditioning and practicing hard, knowing that it would prepare me for the stress and struggle of games. My usual practice partner was perennial All-Pro, Pro Bowler, and future Hall of Famer Howie Long. This man was an animal. He possessed a little something extra that elevated his game to another plane. In addition to his power and unmatched intensity, he was both physically and mentally quick, with the ability to pivot to plan B or C on a dime. To say that he kept me and many others on their toes would be an understatement. But I was grateful to have him as a practice partner, as he forced me to heighten my reflexes and up my game.

With Howie and Max

There was never much small talk during practice—just strap it on, go to work, and know when to back off at the end of a play. Every Wednesday was deemed offense day when the defense offered a look at what we would face from our opponents in the upcoming game. During these drills, the initial steps were always at full speed to establish contact and then get our heads and hands in the right spots. If we didn't throttle back quickly after that, it wouldn't end well. This was learned from endless hours of banging and watching a few guys go too far.

But every so often, someone had a bad day and crossed over the thin line that would inevitably end with a little push away and a visual or verbal warning. And then there was the one practice where the line was blown to pieces. Howie just had an epidural injection in his spine and was feeling a little edgy when our center, Bill Lewis, got a lot more than a preview. Tempers ran short when Bill told Howie to fuck off at the end of a play. Everything came to a halt as we prepared for the other shoe to drop.

Howie snapped back, "What did you just say?" There was a collective sigh among the players and coaches in earshot as everyone knew what was coming, and it wouldn't be good for Bill. In the best-case scenario, he would be maimed, but there was always the worst case to consider, too. In a flash, Howie figuratively left the building. He morphed into a typhoon of rage, and before Bill got a response out of his lips, he was fast asleep.

It was akin to watching a high-rise implosion. Bill found himself on the wrong end of a Mike Tyson-style uppercut that looked like a cap popping off a well-shaken Coke. Shit was flying everywhere. Bill's mouthguard flew one way, his helmet another, and his two front teeth pierced through his bottom lip, all in less than a second. Howie got in some hot water for damaging Al Davis's product, while Bill, with mouth stitches secured, rejoined practice without uttering another word. I suspect the bad blood would persist throughout the season in any other profession, but not in football. These two were joking around before the next game, as everyone recognized that the aggression was sometimes a challenge to contain. It was just part of the business.

Like it or not, these mentally and physically exhausting practices would always end with ten one-hundred-yard dashes. I usually joined the linebackers and running backs to avoid my linemates yelling at me to slow down. It was poor form to make my teammates look bad, but what can I say? I was a racehorse, remember? I loved the exertion and found sick pleasure in leaving any last energy on the field. It helped me tremendously during games since I could compensate for skill deficits with my stamina. I knew I had my opponent when we would break the huddle to see him leaning on his knees, still fighting to catch his breath.

My conditioning only picked up in the offseasons when I planted myself at my home away from home: Gold's Gym in Venice, California. My Raiders' jersey, "Wright 66," proudly hangs on the bottom row as a foundation for all the jerseys above. It's an honor to see it there after all the years of sweat, blood, and more than a few loads of vomit left in the mecca of bodybuilding. I lived nearby in Marina del Rey, so spending two or three hours pumping weights every day was easy. I loved the space with its massive open rooms, elite trainers, the widest variety of equipment, and all the local loony tunes making it entertaining. One of my first trainers was renowned nutritionist Dr. Phillip Goglia before he was deemed an expert in his field. He trained me, and his wife prepared all my meals. They guided me to a solid 300 pounds that could bench press 500 pounds and run the 40-yard dash in 4.85 seconds. With their help, I hit my prime.

I worked one body part for two hours straight once a week to tear down the fibers and then allowed them six days to build and recover. Many mornings, I took one big hit of herb to help achieve the extreme focus needed for the next couple of hours of pounding weights. Phillip knew how to get results, and I had the relentless drive to follow his instructions. To be clear, though, the herb was my idea. While some people smoke to get high, a hit before a gym session always worked for me.

I joined the team in 1987 and found my first order of business was to march in a picket line as the entire league went on strike. This unforeseen turn of events allowed me to bond with many of my new teammates. Some were jovial, while others were clouded by frustration over walking a picket line instead of picking up their game check.

Picket Line with John Clay, Raiders #1 Draft Pick

One such massive character was light on reciprocal conversation, but I pressed on sharing how I played right tackle and was eager to help the line. "How about you?" I asked, hoping to forge a new connection.

With zero effect, he paused, looked me up and down, and gave a measured response: "I'm the veteran All-Pro right tackle, Henry Lawrence."

I swallowed hard. Shit, I was here to try and take his starting position. It would require more than a few hours for me to extract the foot I just stuck in my mouth.

Then he added, "My buddies call me Killer, but you can call me Henry," followed by a prolonged, unblinking stare. Out of the corner of my eye, I caught a few Raiders snickering as they observed what a mess I made of my introduction.

After that awkward encounter, I kept the conversation light on the picket line. I was also distracted by the second-floor offices where owner Al Davis and the staff stood in the window looking down on us week after week. Slowly but surely, teammates disappeared from the line as they lost hope. Once I found myself among a handful of players still carrying signs and slogging in endless circles, I decided to throw in my sign and jump on the next flight to Phoenix to see my folks.

It felt so good to get away from everything: the stress of picketing in front of my new team office and the media constantly seeking comments, hoping to publish something that could only get me in trouble. I was far away from all the drama when I sat down for dinner. Just as we started to eat, the phone rang like an unwanted alarm.

"Steve, it's Al LoCasale," the fast-talking head assistant to Raiders owner Al Davis. "Mr. Davis wants you back right away, and he means it. He'll increase your salary by twenty-five percent and give you a guarantee."

"Thanks, Al, but I'm in the middle of dinner with my folks. I'll call you back tomorrow," I said.

After no more than five minutes, the phone rang again. "Damn it, Steve, Mr. Davis will guarantee fifty percent of your contract if you come back right now."

Again, I thanked him with a noncommittal tone and said I would call back in the morning. Now my parents and I were starting to get a little entertainment out of this game. Back to the table we went, cracking another round of beers when the phone rang a third time, and Dad grinned. "This is getting good," he beamed with pride, rubbing his hands together in giddy anticipation.

"Steve, Mr. Davis is raising the offer and guarantying one hundred percent of it if you're back here to practice first thing in the morning," Al said with urgency. He was nearly pleading at this point. I sensed that he had orders to make this deal happen no matter what it took.

With my best courtroom lawyer voice, I paused and said, "Listen to this, Al," as I put the phone by my plate, dropping my fork so he could hear the bang as it struck the table. "I'm on my way," I said, and I meant it. I shoveled the last few bites of food, drained my beer, and headed to the airport to catch the first flight back to Los Angeles. That was a memorable dinner with my folks; we laughed about it many times. My kind of luck to be negotiating the best contract of my career in under fifteen minutes.

When I returned to Los Angeles and pulled into the Raiders' training facility, I met a crowd at the entrance. Much to my surprise, some teammates were back picketing and blocking my path. I nodded and motioned with a peace sign, but they scowled at me out of sheer frustration. They realized I was the latest scab. Driving into the parking lot was uncomfortable, but after twenty-four days of striking, the dam was breaking, and many players were on the verge of rejoining. By that afternoon, the rest of the team crossed the line, and the strike was officially over. Team tensions ran high that season with a few extra scuffles during practice, but it never carried over off the field.

Along with frustrations over the strike, other antagonisms were kept to the turf, which was especially important when I shared a room with my opponent during training camp. My roommate was defensive end Pete Koch, who I genuinely liked. I faced him daily in mano a mano drills that were everyone's favorite. It was raw competition with a clear winner and loser in front of everyone, including the decision-makers. I was in my prime, but nothing was guaranteed during camp. These battles took place under the brutal sun, testing my patience. More often than not, it would end with Pete and I rolling around and grabbing each other's face masks. Then we would throw punches until we were separated. Once up and held back, hypermasculinity posturing followed with a few nasty words. It was just a part of the job.

After our morning disagreement and lunch, Pete and I would head back to our room to watch *Bonanza* on the couch or nap before afternoon practice. Then, just like *Groundhog Day*, we would be at it again: roommates and friends, until we hit the turf.

As we got back into the practice and game rhythm of the regular season, I had a chance to observe this infamous crew in action. It was a team like no other. I got to appreciate this on another level before an early-season game. Everyone was in the locker room taping up, pounding coffee, and doing whatever else they needed to get game ready. One of our stalwart linebackers decided to keep the pregame mood light and loose. He was a leader who was loved and respected, along with being the funniest guy on the team. He was known to say and do things that dropped you back with bellyaching laughter.

Motown soul classics got him going and shaking loose. On this day, his passion was full tilt as he worked out the pregame angst. He moved, grooved, and climbed the table in the middle of the locker room, buck naked, grabbing his schlong and swinging it without missing a beat. It was remarkably out of the norm, especially before a professional football game. I was used to the Cowboys and Colts, where the mood was serious and focused.

Any pregame jitters disappeared as teammates shook their heads and laughed. Just then, Head Coach Art Shell entered directly behind our table dancer. Our entertainer must've picked up on the nonverbal cues, spinning around to meet eyes with his boss. Coach stared him down while none of us dared to open our mouths. He made a split-second decision and then burst out with the loudest laugh. As he bent over, unable to hold back, our private dancer jumped down, and we continued prepping for the game as if it never happened. I could see and feel the togetherness, lightness, and crazy energy building and bonding us all. We were a solid brotherhood, and everyone could feel it. I don't recall whom we played that day, but I know we won because the drinks poured freely on the flight back to Los Angeles as we joked about the event in the locker room while blasting the tunes and playing cards.

Greg Townsend and Sean Jones, our massive, cool Jamaican defensive end, usually controlled pregame music. The defensive DJs always kept the locker room grooving with a portable boombox that offered a range of Motown and funk. During one pregame episode, the music ended abruptly, so a rookie took the opportunity to drop in a disk from his collection. It wasn't our Motown or funk. I could feel the awkward energy building. Everyone kept to the business of getting ready, but when the music turned into nails on a chalkboard, Sean strolled out of the training room and over to the box. He mechanically ejected the disk, took a long look at it, and threw it like a frisbee into the cinder block wall, shattering it into pieces. Then he slid in a Motown favorite and strutted back to his locker. No one laughed, cheered, or even acknowledged it. The mood and energy were back. I glanced at the rookie to see how he managed the public shaming. He just dropped his head and knew not to say a word. One of his fellow rooks gave him a conciliatory pat on the back as he passed by, heading for the trainer's room.

Each player brought their unique pregame rituals to the locker room, both good and bad. I learned about the unsavory side rather early in my rookie year. We had just finished our warm-up for the first home game against our archrivals, the Washington Redskins. I was on pins and needles as I sprinted up the tunnel for final locker room preparations before kickoff. Assuming I was the first one in, I lined up to the empty row of urinals and noticed a pair of cleats facing the toilet in the adjacent stall. I registered the oddity but then heard the all-too-familiar snort of someone sucking up a fair bit of cocaine. The player peeked over the stall to ensure the coast was clear, gave me a wink, and ducked back down to finish his business. Sure, I partied with the best of them in the offseason, but to witness this before a game was a huge letdown. It was certainly not something I expected from America's team, but I suppose they don't put that type of thing in the brochures.

By the time I hit veteran status, my pregame pattern was to arrive at least three hours before kickoff with most of the other linemen. We were often the earliest to get our ankles taped and spend time on the field. The stadium was empty at this point, and we would sit on the bench reviewing audible calls to stay in lockstep.

Next, I strolled back into the locker room to crank up Metallica's "Enter Sandman" and tape my knuckles to prevent them from coming out during hits and grabs. To further prepare my mind, I conjured up ugly memories and fictional stories, all intended to generate intense anger. Imagine forcing yourself to this point of rage brought on by the most wicked thoughts conceivable. I wouldn't even recognize myself in the mirror before a game because I looked like a padded-up serial killer. By the time we took the field, I would have sweat dripping off my chin and was ready to fight with a froth in my mouth. That was the sign that I was all in and prepared to battle. If that process wouldn't wear on a person over time, I'm not sure what would.

Game Face

The locker room was a world of its own as a highly coveted and protected space for players. Even coaches rarely strolled through, and when they did, it was to talk business, and then they kept it moving. Front office personnel were also seldom spotted in the sanctum. When they scurried in, they were on a mission to get a ball signed for some high-dollar fan before sliding out with their heads down. Then there was the media. They flooded in after games to disrupt the brotherly time of celebration or defeat but otherwise were persona non grata, much to the relief of players. The need for a safeguarded space was understood since players were constantly under a microscope outside of the locker room. Most of the field time was videotaped, and press days meant that reporters were on players like drug-sniffing dogs probing for anything newsworthy. It got tiresome quickly.

In the face of all the pressures outside, whatever was said and done in the locker and training rooms stayed there. This was where the brotherhood shined. If there was an issue between guys, it was resolved in the locker room for everyone's sake. Family disputes would eat us up if they persisted. However, there was a more sinister side to the space that was rarely discussed. This was where the sick and lame healed miraculously and were sent back onto the field. The medicine was not magical, but it certainly seemed that way when the 2023 Super Bowl Champion and MVP Patrick Mahomes sprinted out of the locker room after halftime and scrambled for his longest run of the day. All this high performance after hobbling into the locker room at halftime? "Extra time for treatment" was the collective storyline from the Kansas City sideline. Meanwhile, you could hear a pin drop among commentators in response to that explanation. What? It was the perfect moment for sportscaster Chris Berman to bark his famous one-liner: C'mon man.

Over the course of my eleven years with four teams, I witnessed plenty of unconventional locker room treatments. My jaw dropped after one incident in the training room when a teammate assisted in straightening a player's leg post-knee surgery. With one sudden movement, he came down with 300 pounds of force. The player screamed in agony, and the trainer lost his shit as panic ensued. Everyone was in shock. This wasn't a medically approved approach to breaking down scar tissue, but damn, it actually worked. It freed the impingement that had been slowing his recovery.

Beyond the training room, I had one questionable team doctor who followed players around the lockers like an alleyway dealer, offering shots to numb the pain or get ahead of any potential discomfort. This archaic medical professional would have at least a half dozen hypodermic needles at the ready with a cocktail of numbing drugs poised to stick anyone that showed tepid interest. I agreed to these offerings a few times for deep thigh bruises but never for joint pain. Another like-minded doctor would fish assorted pills out of a large mason jar with conviction about what ailed me. With the stakes high to stay healthy and on the payroll, it was easy to accept whatever it took to stay on the field.

No matter the injury or pain, you couldn't drag one of my tough fellow linemates, Kurt Marsh, off the field. But he paid a heavy price for it. He was featured on *60 Minutes* for a tragic foot amputation resulting from reoccurring trauma and using painkillers to override his body's alarm system. Short-term gains for long-term pains were rarely my mode of operation. As crazy as it sounds, I wanted to feel the pain, recognize the discomfort, and let my body judge its capabilities. The football field was where I became in tune with my body, when and how much to push it, and it kept me on a healthy path.

Given what was expected on game day, it wasn't unreasonable to seek other more natural stabilizers in anticipation of the work that lay ahead. When we were on the road, we had a strict eleven o'clock curfew with absolutely no visitors . . . meaning no girls in the rooms. I was worn out on one road trip to Miami, and some coaches took note. I was dead set on having company that night, dropping my room number into a girl's purse in the lobby before heading to my bed. I gave up by 11:30 p.m. and was comatose when I heard the door open ajar.

"Get her out of here by 1," whispered my short-straw-drawing night watchman assistant coach with his deep Southern drawl. I heard a girl giggle as her voluptuous silhouette slipped by him and his spare keys into my room. We didn't acknowledge the rule-bending that night other than a brief fist bump before I took the field at Joe Robbie Stadium the following day. I played with more energy than I had in weeks. Sometimes coaches know you better than you realize.

Early in my Raiders career, I acquired a nickname that I never shook. As I walked into the training room to get my ankles taped for practice one morning, the head trainer, George Anderson, shouted at me, "Get on the table, Doc!"

"Huh?" I said, bemused.

George proceeded to tell me my name was Doc. "It's settled," he said.

I was scratching my head to understand what he was talking about when he pointed to a full-page cartoon taped to the wall. It was a picture of a curly-headed stud selling orgasms from his delivery bike. Someone took a black Sharpie and wrote "Steve Wright" across his chest. But I wasn't all about the ladies, at least not as much as the cartoon suggested. I remember an afternoon practice when a strippergram showed up in our locker room to sing happy birthday, but I was too exhausted to pay attention. As I looked up, I noticed that our team of fifty naked dudes were taking showers, getting dressed, and going about their business as if she wasn't even there. Like any employee at the end of a long day, we were too tired to care. We just wanted to get home.

Outside the locker room, friends and strangers at bars sought the scoop on the Raiders' cheerleading squad, The Raiderettes. Who was available? Which ones did I date? To set the record straight, the one and only Raiderette that I dated was Linda, a saucy brunette with big Hollywood dreams. Dating cheerleaders wasn't a concern for the front office, unlike the Cowboys, but other Raiderettes dismissed me. Once I was dating Linda, I was a dead fish to the rest . . . steer clear of Wright. She left me high and dry for fame, but I recovered and regained fresh-fish status. Truth be told, I became more of a big brother to those babes than anything else.

Beyond the cheerleaders, plenty of entertaining doors opened because of football. While I was never one for video games, *Madden NFL* was a big deal in the early 1990s when I was asked to support its marketing as it launched across Europe. It was well timed during the offseason, while the compensation and first-rate travel made it an opportunity I couldn't refuse. Along with a few other players, I spent time in London, Amsterdam, Frankfurt, Cologne, and Paris, signing autographs and talking up the game.

While in London, I accepted a guest spot on the *BBC*'s Monday Night Football broadcast to provide color and occupy halftime. It was so much fun to ham it up on camera and test my commentary skills. As it turns out, I'm much better on the line than in front of the camera. But it was a great way to explore and remind myself where I shined.

After first-class living and traveling in Europe, I returned to reality as I entered the locker room the following season. When I hit the showers, I was reminded how nasty they could be with bloody gauze, athletic tape, and chunks of sod clogging the drains. As foul and unhygienic as it was, it got even nastier when teammates broke the sacred rule and peed in the shower. While this tenet made sense on face value alone, it took on added significance when I trudged through murky ankle-deep water.

One of my teammates was a serious germophobe, so the locker room was a true test of his will. He came into this backed-up sewer of a shower wearing Gucci flip-flops and carrying a toiletry bag with two plush towels. He would methodically lay one towel down as a barrier against the germs lining the sink and then carefully place the articles from his bag on top. But the worst step of the process awaited him. He flinched as he tip-toed through five inches of toxic waste, followed by the fastest shower I've ever witnessed. I guess he reasoned that if he moved quickly, maybe he could avoid picking up a viral hitchhiker.

As I was soaping up and trying to ignore the rogue boogers cemented to the shower wall, I turned to see Sick Mick eating a cheeseburger on the open toilet without a care in the world.

"What the fuck are you looking at?" He laughed.

"How hungry do you have to be?" I playfully shouted back. I could appreciate his intent to keep weight on no matter what it took, but come on, man, that was just wrong.

I was one of the lighter offensive linemen starting the season at 295 pounds, and there was plenty of pressure to maintain the mass throughout the season. We would weigh in every Thursday after practice, and as the season progressed, it grew increasingly difficult to keep on the weight. I dropped closer to 280 pounds. By mid-season, I started sliding weight plates into the back of my shorts before weighing in, eventually graduating from a two-and-a-half-pound plate to a ten-pound plate by the end of the season. The trainers were on to my scheme but just shook their heads as they recorded my inaccurate poundage.

I needed to keep my body weight up because it was an insurance policy against the big hits, or so I liked to believe. That said, I still endured my share of steamrollers. It would chip at my confidence when I lost a mano a mano battle in a game, especially if it was an off day. I had my tricks for getting back on track, positive self-talk and the like, but nothing seemed to work at the outset of one contest against the Giants. It was my introduction to playing left tackle after our regular guy went down in practice. Lucky me, I drew the card to start against future Hall of Famer Lawrence Taylor "LT" in the Meadowlands. And I had little time to prepare.

When I took to the field to battle the all-world LT, he was already strutting around, amped up, yelling shit in my direction. "Wright, you're in for a long fucking day." He was spot on, but I couldn't let my nerves show. LT was the complete package, unlike anyone I had battled up to that point in my career.

The first play of the game had our quarterback Steve Beuerlein take a deep drop to throw a long ball. LT planted his helmet into my chest, driving me back on my heels until both of us ran over Beurerlein, making quick work of everything in his path. I had a come-to-Jesus moment knowing I'd better get my shit together fast, or I was in for a long, miserable day at the office.

As the leader of the offense, Steve Beuerlein knew exactly what to do. Before the next play, he shook his head and pulled me close so only I could hear. "Looks like it's time for you to kick his ass." He pushed me back, rattling off the play to the rest of the offense.

As the huddle broke, I nodded my appreciation toward Steve, who flashed a knowing smile. He could've berated me in front of the offense, but he was a natural leader who understood how to motivate his teammates. He knew that I thrived on encouragement, hating to let anyone down. I was a team guy in the fabric of my being, and my guys could rely on me just like I could depend on them. His words made all the difference in that pivotal moment. It worked like magic as I settled in for an afternoon battle against one of the all-time best. It turned out to be an excellent game for me due, in part, to Steve.

While the quarterback serves as the field coach, as veterans, we were sometimes asked to watch over a rookie, especially high draft picks. These guys came into the league weighted down with heavy expectations and plenty of money coming their way. While they excelled at the college level, they now faced a more challenging game with bigger, stronger, and faster players and higher stakes to match. Yet they were just kids trying to fit in whenever I peeled away all the bravado.

One year, I was asked to keep an eye on a local star who showed strong potential. While his college record was impressive, he carried plenty of off-field demons. After our first morning practice session, we decided to break bread off-site, and he rolled up to my car reeking of marijuana. I loved my herb, too, but there was a time and place for everything, and the first week of camp wasn't it. I sensed he might be in for a bumpy ride.

We hit the bank on our way to lunch, where he fiddled around in his pocket as if looking for spare change. After an awkward minute at the teller counter, he pulled out a wadded-up clump that must've served as a bar napkin, given its condition. As it turns out, it was a check for $350,000. The cashier and I gasped in unison. The flighty treatment of such a large sum blew my mind, as all he wanted was twenty dollars of cash for lunch.

Another veteran shared a similar story with a rookie he took under his wing that same year. While helping carry his bags, he discovered a check for $770,000 tossed alongside candy wrappers in the recesses of the kid's truck. All the rookie said was "Ah, man, I've been looking for that," as he collected it along with a half-eaten Snickers bar.

While most of us didn't enter the league with money, something about the environment distorted most players' financial management practices. It was an alternate reality with plenty of cash flying around, so players started to believe there was a never-ending supply. As careers abruptly ended or slowly fizzled, a hard lesson accompanied the fall. Like all things in life, the time on the field and compensation were finite. Yet, with plenty of resources at the ready, it's still far too common to hear about wealthy athletes going broke in retirement. If managed correctly, nearly all these guys could spend the rest of their lives never worrying about a cent.

This haphazard treatment of fleeting wealth wasn't only a rookie problem, as many seasoned veterans could induce shock and awe with their reckless behavior. In one case, a middle linebacker's neglect of his ride was born out of sheer panic. During our pregame preparations, I noticed his vacant locker, which was highly unusual this close to game time. With less than an hour to spare, he raced into the locker room, dressed in a full suit with sweat trickling from his chin. I was relieved to see him, knowing there must be a story behind his extraordinary lateness. As it turned out, he was stuck in a horrible traffic jam leading to the Coliseum as the clock ticked to game time. In sheer desperation, he did the only thing he could to arrive before the whistle blew. He begged two random guys on the street, throwing them his keys. He asked them to deliver his gridlocked new Mercedes to the stadium parking lot while he sprinted the last ten blocks. Many of us put a wager on whether his car would show up. But, defying all odds placed on human behavior, the gamble worked out in his favor. Humanity prevailed. He was ready for kickoff, and meanwhile, the two dudes waited patiently in the parking lot with his new car.

This linebacker was resourceful but had another funny habit that revealed itself beyond taking risks with his ride. Before our next game, I discovered him in a panic as he scoured his locker, throwing all contents onto the floor. He couldn't find his lucky rock that was supposed to be on the top shelf against the edge of the cloth where he always positioned it. I guess he was just a wee bit superstitious. He managed through the game and then got the coach's clearance to miss Monday's film session. He had to take care of personal business. He split for Big Bear in the San Bernardino Mountains directly after the game, leaving his teammates and family behind on a quest to find another lucky rock. I can't imagine another NFL team so deftly managing this insane asylum. Fortunately for his family and us, he returned to practice the next day smiling. He had a new rock properly resting in his locker right where it was supposed to be.

Beyond our locker room and even the Raiders stadium, there was much more worth sharing and perhaps even more colorful. The place was packed with rabid fans worthy of the *Mad Max* movie set: eyepatches, spiked helmets, crazy painted faces, and leather Raiders jackets. Quite the collection of characters, but they loved us and wore it all with unmatched pageantry and lunacy.

One Sunday, I had to sit out a game and meandered through the parking lot with my parents to witness the pregame tailgate scene firsthand. For those few hours, it was one big circus with everyone getting along unless a fool with a Denver Broncos jersey dared to venture through the lot. If you wore Raiders' gear, you were a member of the tribe. This went for the notorious Bloods and Crips' gangs too. They checked their hate at the gates and managed to stay cool as long as they remained separated . . . at least until the game ended and they were back out onto Martin Luther King Boulevard.

The infamous boulevard headed east of the Coliseum wasn't for amateurs or tourists. I learned this the hard way after my first game with the Raiders when I exited left instead of right as I departed the stadium. I rode my Cowboy-blue convertible east under the 110 freeway into Vermont Knolls, Watts, and Gramercy Park, sticking out like a beacon of white privilege.

A cop car pulled up alongside me and shouted, "Where the fuck are you going, big guy?"

I flashed a high-beam grin and said, "Heading to the beach," as I was still basking in the glory of a win over the Broncos.

The officer frowned as he flicked on his lights and sirens and yelled at me to follow him as he ripped a U-turn on the busy thoroughfare. As we passed back under the 110, he waved me up beside him, commanding, "Go that way, and don't come back!"

I was dying to say that I had a lot of Blood and Crip friends back in the stadium lot, but this wasn't a time to joke around. So instead, I cruised home, top down with the sun baking my windshield as I headed west for the beach. It was strange to have two worlds butt up against each other, but it wasn't the first or last time the contrast was so apparent.

Racial tensions were high and building throughout the Los Angeles area in the early 1990s, yet I never felt any of this in the Raiders' locker room. Sports teams were expected to drop politics, religion, race, or anything else controversial at the door. We fought for each other, not against one another; it was that simple. I appreciated that every player was treated with a baseline of respect, minus the rookies, but I also recognized the importance of athletes using their visibility to address issues of social importance. I respect the hell out of Colin Kaepernick and honor his sacrifice to bring attention and conversation to critical racial injustice issues. In my view, we need more Colin Kaepernicks in today's world.

I'm not sure how we managed to maintain the sanctity of our locker room back then, given the tension surrounding us. I recall it starting with the Los Angeles Police Chief Daryl Gates and his excessive use of force against the Black community. He called it Operation Hammer, and the name described it well. Meanwhile, some Koreans and Blacks got ugly with one another while the media fed the fire to up their ratings. Everyone saw Rodney King's beating, which would surely lead to jail time for the four cops and bring some calm to a city on edge. When the dirty cops were acquitted, there was a moment of shock, and then the city ignited.

Once I heard the news, I loaded my convertible and scrambled to get out of town, assuming things would turn violent. I jumped on the elevated 10 freeway, cutting straight through the center of Los Angeles en route to the desert. It was midday on April 29, 1992, as I slowed on an unusually quiet freeway to watch the fires and pockets of billowing smoke to my left and right as sirens blared in the background. The riots persisted for six days until five thousand Federal troops squashed the unrest. But not before sixty-three unnecessary deaths and twelve thousand arrests. It was awful, every bit of it: from the horrific beating of Rodney King to the dismissal of the cops and the wake of destruction that followed. It made me reflect on how fortunate I was and how much work remained to make this world a better place for all. It sickened me, but I was unsure how to respond privately and publicly. I focused on treating everyone fairly, hoping each small act could build a domino effect of concern and compassion for everyone, regardless of race. Gandhi's "Be the change" became one of my mantras and is something I still repeat during meditations.

While the mood was often light around the Raiders' locker room, the seriousness of fights and injuries on the field was sobering. I got into an intense battle with the Chief's nose guard, Bill Moss, that turned into a bench-clearing brawl ending in Moss's ejection from the game and me with the mouth of Skeletor from *Masters of the Universe*. I bled so badly that our team doctor, Rob Huizenga, would recall the scene in his book, *You're Okay, It's Just a Bruise* for the gruesome nature of the injury.

It all started rather innocently as I chopped Bill on a pass play. He latched onto my leg and wouldn't let go, so we rose and locked face masks like two beasts unwilling to give an inch. Bodies banged, fists flew, and benches emptied. I caught what felt like a sledgehammer under my chin, sending my helmet flying. To make matters worse, blood was flowing down my face fast, so I knew it was more than just a minor injury. I went straight into the training room to discover that the length of my front gum was completely sheered. It revealed a fully recessed gum, exposing the roots of my front teeth. Beyond grisly, it was made worse by the doubling of my blood as it mixed with saliva. I took one look in the mirror and decided there would be no chips and hot salsa for me that night.

A patch job by the team doctor included a couple of injections of the 'caine brothers (novocaine, xylocaine, and lidocaine) and tweezers to pull my gums down like a window blind. The quick fix got me back in the game, but every time I leaned into my stance, blood would froth from my mouth.

I noticed some guys wincing and pointing at me during the huddle. "Doc, that's just not right," my linemate Max chimed in as I spewed blood. Max was a true warrior, so it had to be gnarly if he was concerned enough to say something.

After the game, the team doctor numbed me again, grabbed the sutures, and cleaned up a mouth that belonged on a horror movie set, not in a football locker room. To this day, my gum still shows evidence of that traumatic injury.

Managing pain should be part of the job description in the NFL, right alongside harnessing aggression. I recall staggering into a huddle, convinced I had fractured my shin. It was actually a massive lump from a helmet, and when I showed it to Max, he laughed and shook his head before breaking the huddle. This was the first time I had my bare shin hit this way. On the very next play, another guy hit the lump dead on and smashed it flat. It hurt so bad that it made my eyes roll back. After the play, I limped back to the huddle, showing Max again.

This time, he shook his head, laughing even harder. "Problem solved, Doc." That was just another day at the office.

With Max

Unfortunately, I bore witness to far too many injuries that still make my stomach churn. In fact, football is the only profession with a one-hundred-percent injury rate, and I witnessed my fair share. The Cowboys' defensive tackle, John Dutton, was a warrior I passed coming off the field during one of my first games in the league when I froze in my tracks, noticing something askew. His eye was literally hanging out of the socket. It was horrifying to watch as he lost his equilibrium, staggering toward the sideline. He screamed for help, grabbing for his eye. He knew, based on our reaction, that his injury was truly horrifying. John didn't lose his sight that day, which was nothing short of a miracle. I, on the other hand, nearly lost my lunch.

And then there was Steve "Smitty" Smith, the Raiders beloved fullback from Penn State, who trotted off the field holding his hand more gently than a newborn. When he opened his cradled paw, I almost threw up. He was out catching balls, and between the tight spiral and the velocity at which it was thrown, the ball split the middle and ring fingers apart. It exposed over an inch of bone and raw meat. He covered it back up, reappearing from the training room about fifteen minutes later for practice with a clubhand. That man was tough.

This was followed by a game in New Orleans when we all heard a loud snap within the interior line. Charlie Hannah, one of our Raiders guards, screamed and attempted to get up when a couple of teammates—as well as our opponents—held him down, given the severity of the injury. His shin literally snapped. His foot was now positioned next to his knee, pointing outward like a discarded toy. It was more akin to a war injury than something you should see in a football game. Not surprisingly, it was a career-ending injury. It was tough to see guys in their prime taken out at the knees, or shins, in Charlie's case, and never to return. It may sound insane, but many would do it all over again to play in the NFL as long as they did.

I finally experienced an injury that almost ended my career as well. A human pileup on the field in Kansas City contorted me into the worst possible position with my arm awkwardly extended. It completely blew out my left shoulder joint. I waddled off the field, bent over at the waist, trying to keep the shoulder steady because it was out of the socket, and jammed straight backward.

Back in the locker room, they administered the first shot of morphine, but it was like throwing a plastic dart into a black hole. "Hit me again, fucker," I shouted, still amped up and hitting an eleven out of ten on the pain scale.

"That's all we should do right now," said the assistant, pulling away along with his enormous needle.

"Bullshit, again," I said with a lower but firm, I-mean-fucking-business voice.

Dr. Huizenga leaned into the assistant. "Do it, another shot of morphine. He's 300 pounds, pissed off, and the pain is far from over."

Fortunately, the assistant listened. The next step was to cut me out of my jersey and pads, which took some serious manipulation and patience. Then I was beyond thankful because I didn't feel a thing as they jerked and pulled my shoulder, dropping it back into the socket with an audible thud. I went into surgery the next day back in Los Angeles with Dr. Neal ElAttrache, who said it was the worst shoulder he'd seen. He later earned a fantastic reputation for repairing all kinds of top athletes, including Tom Brady and Kobe Bryant. I got lucky with Dr. Neil because it's holding tight over thirty years later.

Train Wreck on Wright, #66

With all the injuries and pain I witnessed throughout my career, I adopted a prevention mindset that involved trying different approaches to saving my body and extending my career. I was the first of the Raiders to wear a shield over my eyes after seeing and hearing of players getting their eyes poked. Not long after this decision, my linemate and good friend, Don Mosebar, lost his eye on the field. The freak injury ended his illustrious career.

I also wore knee braces in every practice and game beginning in college. Wearing them in training gave me time to adapt and avoid the psychological misconception that they would slow me down. The mind was a powerful tool and could be a weapon if I wasn't careful. I didn't want to give it any room to question this safety measure. There were too many big bodies flying around, tripping, and getting tossed to jeopardize one of them caving in my knee. I went through about half a dozen knee braces over my career. There's a high likelihood that at least one of those bent braces could've been a knee ligament or worse.

My one knee injury occurred in January 1991 in Buffalo while playing the Bills in a crisp negative-thirty degrees. There was nothing that a knee brace could do to save me from snapping my ACL in those frigid temperatures. My ligaments were as tight as piano strings. This was partly due to some lineman antics before the game when my buddy hatched a not-so-bright plan. He cut off all the arms and legs of the thermals, which would've offered some protection from the extreme cold. I guess he assumed the tough-guy look would give us an advantage on the field. Clearly, losing fifty-one to three and getting badly injured didn't work in our favor.

After much research, I decided to have the torn ends removed instead of reconnected. This meant that I needed to build up my hamstring to compensate for the ligament loss. This wise choice worked great. I was running at full speed by the start of training camp the following year.

Now, that was my body, but what about my mind? I toiled in the most inglorious position in football my whole career: in the trench with the offensive line. We performed the yeoman's work for the offense with little praise or accolades if we won but most of the blame if we lost. We were expected to protect our quarterback quietly and effectively so he could throw touchdowns to the flashy wide receivers who danced in the end zone. Alternatively, we were to mash and maul the defense, clearing holes for our high-dollar running backs to rush through for touchdowns under the crowd's roar. All eyes and cameras were on these other positions. Meanwhile, the line fought like pit bulls for every yard. It wasn't uncommon to go unnoticed unless one of us gave up a sack or jumped offside. Despite all that, we loved it. It takes a certain kind of player to be attracted to that type of role.

Locked and Loaded

I'm not a sports psychologist, but after decades in and around sports, I understand what's needed above the shoulders to succeed. These include a few recognizable things like passion, mental toughness, and love of the team, but it also involves less obvious elements such as operating with humility and creating space away from the sport.

I took to sports like a golden retriever takes to water, but my draw to football was the most magnetic. After grade school practice, I would get home and still needed more, so I begged to watch the NFL. Dad, who ran a tight ship, had a cruel habit of turning off *Monday Night Football* at 8:30 p.m. sharp, regardless of the game status. That was truly sacrilegious for anyone passionate about the sport. The announcers made every game an event not to miss. And I was lucky enough to have the same trio call a few of my games over a decade later. It was torture to forgo the last quarter of close matchups, but Dad's house rules weren't up for debate. Even worse, the Viking games my family attended resulted in a nonnegotiable early exit to beat traffic. No matter the score at the start of the fourth quarter, the Wrights were out. These cliffhangers left me begging for more. I dreamed about plays that might've been used during the final minutes of those games. I suppose it was the earliest memory I have of sports visualization.

It was common for me to have afterschool football practice followed by a quick dinner and then off to city league for another round. This was fine with me because I loved every minute of it. From that point on, the more I could play football, the better. Despite my passion and ability, not a single childhood, high school, or college coach ever suggested I had what it took to make it to the NFL. Yet that didn't deter me one bit. I was playing with a pure heart, not an agenda.

It wasn't until age thirty-five that the mental exhaustion of the sport caught up with me. While I still loved the physical aspects of the game, I was finished both mentally and emotionally. This made my departure from the sport necessary. If I had stayed without the passion for the game, I would've put myself and my team at risk.

The pressures of playing in the NFL are immense and derailed many a career. Even with a healthy psychological profile going in, I was challenged from the start. The incessant yelling from my Cowboys' line coach would send my head into a tailspin and rock my confidence until Coach Ditka offered me some mind-bending insight.

"Start worrying if Jim stops yelling at you," Ditka stated definitively during one of our post-practice walks.

"I don't understand. Can't he see I'm giving him all I've got?" I questioned as I fought back my frustration, balling my fists so hard that my fingernails dug into my palms.

"Yup, he does, but he also sees more in you than you see in yourself," Ditka said as he paused to look me in the eyes. "Trust the process, Steve; he knows what he's doing."

In that instance, a stifling burden I carried in my mind was set free. *They really saw a lot in me?* Within a millisecond, I felt light as air. I grinned at Ditka, shaking my head. I had much to learn about the mental fortitude needed to thrive in this profession.

I learned to manage conflicting emotions and intensity on the practice field. But it became more complex hours before a game and would crescendo at the first snap of the ball. The pregame mental gymnastics were an out-of-body ritual. One of my Pro Bowl linemates, who will remain nameless, cried before games because he was so mentally cranked. Other players puked or punched lockers before entering the Coliseum . . . and these guys were all seasoned professionals.

The temperature and stress mounted as I paced around the echoing tunnel to take the field. My dark emotions had nowhere to escape in the confines of the tight space. The ambient energy felt like tiny electric shocks as I bolted through a lineup of cheerleaders into a sold-out stadium as my name flooded the soundwaves.

Modern-Day Gladiators at the Coliseum

Even a decade into my career, this pregame introduction ritual was a mind-distorting experience. I shouted obscenities, threw my body around, and pounded on my teammates as the caffeine and testosterone redlined. The bubbling rage made me feel indestructible. But I always tried to remember Lao Tzu's wise adage: "The best fighter is never angry." While pressure filled my world, I worked to manage my voltage. I had to stay under control so it would peak on the first snap of the ball.

Controlled Rage

The first play of the game was an internal firework display that began with the finale. Mental strain finally had a release valve pointed directly at my opponent. It was challenging to maintain, but I couldn't let my intensity wane. Whether provoked or unprovoked, I had to bring it all or risk losing my job.

When provoked, retaliation would get me tossed out of the

game. This is where bounties had their place. When an opposing player took a cheap shot at one of our guys, each lineman tossed in five bucks for the player who could "de-cleate" our target the next time we played. I had to blow him off his cleats for it to count.

As they say, though, what comes around goes around. I was "de-cleated" a few times over the years, and it was never pretty. I felt the bullseye on my earhole. And I kept my head swiveling to stay alert for these highly paid hitmen. It messed with my mind: all part of the design. But this is where embracing my killer instincts saved me. I had to believe I was impervious to pain and could handle anything.

Hit and Run "De-cleater"

While I needed to look out for myself, at my core, I'm a team guy who's wired to connect and bond with others. It always filled my cup when I felt a group gelling and reaching a higher performance level as a team. Some of this was nature-derived, but nurturing this instinct solidified its position in my hierarchy of needs. I was taught early that sometimes the team involved self-sacrifice for the good of the whole, which was an easy sell when I was a kid because I was playing with my best friends. We all hung tight in and outside of football. Those bonds were worthy of protection, even if it meant staying on the sideline for a play and missing the action. The high priority of the team and those connections carried up through my time in the NFL. And I wasn't alone in this regard.

Our Raiders quarterback Jim Plunkett shared in these values, requiring that we attend Thursday night camaraderie sessions at Ponchos restaurant in Manhattan Beach after practice. This wasn't about drinking, though tequila shots did find their way onto the tables now and then. This was about staying close to one another, being there, laughing, listening, and connecting. There was no discussion of football, just life. This bonding time went a long way toward our success as a team.

There was a deliberate triage approach to team cohesiveness. It began with the front office, which played an important role in the selection of talent that had to integrate smoothly. The coaches then incorporated observations into their ongoing assessment of team chemistry while the team captains and players worked in tandem to get the misfits going in the same direction or get them out. It was a delicate dance, taking vigilance at all levels to make it work.

Meeting of the Minds and Muscle

While I respected Raiders owner Al Davis, he had his own perspective on what was needed to be successful. He lived in the NFL pressure cooker right along with us, but it permeated his life around the clock for decades. It affected everything about the Raiders, and sometimes not for the better, in my opinion. He was rarely absent from our practice sidelines, where he was seen eyeballing plays. Often, he overrode coaches listing the plays he wanted to see in a game... with zero compromises. It seemed like he carried his *must-win* obsession home, as I learned that he called coaches into the wee hours. He wanted answers to issues he pondered while incessantly combing through practice videos.

I always described Al as hating to talk about football. There was *football* talk, and then there was *dominating football* conversation. They were light-years apart. He'd only welcome you into his tight orbit if you could articulate exactly how you were going to crush your opponent. To call him single-mindedly focused on winning was putting it too lightly. I brought my father into the locker room after a big win at the Coliseum one Sunday afternoon when spirits were high. I thought this would be a safe time to introduce Dad to Al. I was dead wrong. My father stuck his hand out, and Al blew past with a nod, leaving him hanging. He was beelining it to some poor player who was about to get his ass chewed despite the overwhelming victory. Dad took the brush-off in stride with a hardy laugh. Nothing was going to ruin this experience, not even Al's ire.

To be an effective part of the team, I also learned how to eat my share of humble pie. It helped that I played positions that never got the glory, so none was expected when I hit the NFL. In contrast, I watched plenty of egos and attitudes shorten careers. In most cases, they failed to check themselves and learn from their mistakes.

Whenever I screwed up, I owned it, absorbed the lesson, and moved on. . . . Thank you, Mike Ditka. It was inevitable to lose some battles during the three hours of play, but I saw the big picture in winning the war. If I stayed humble and learned the necessary lessons, I could keep my head in check.

I was fortunate to play with Bo Jackson while with the Raiders. Bo, who was a living legend in the football world, was one of the humblest men I knew. All he wanted to do was run with the ball in the game, nothing less and nothing more. One day while we sat around the locker room, the ever-jovial weight and conditioning coach, John "Mother" Dunn, stomped into the locker room and dictated, "Get your asses in the weight room now!"

Bo turned around to face Dunn and smiled. "Fuck you, Mother," he said playfully.

Without missing a beat, Mother laughed and corrected himself. "Okay, everybody but Bo, get your asses in the weight room," he said, giving Bo a wink.

We all headed that way laughing, and Bo hung behind to call it a day. He would save his energy and talents for the game. No one else was that naturally gifted.

I played right tackle for many of Bo's astonishing runs, including a ninety-one-yarder in Seattle and an eighty-eight-yarder at the Colosseum. But after witnessing so many of these untouchable sprints, we started ribbing him about running to avoid contact. "When are you going to hit someone and run them over?" players would ask, and I could sense the pressure building. The next week, we hosted the Denver Broncos. On third and long, Bo blew through the line with only Mike Harden between him and six points. Normally, Bo would hit another gear and fly by, but instead, he put his head down, barreling over Harden. He offered up one of the most brutal hit-and-runs I had ever witnessed.

Harden was tough, but no one could stop the bullet train. He landed on his ass and then his back as Bo planted one foot on his chest and never broke stride. Even Bo seemed to enjoy the demolition work as he strutted the sideline. He relished giving shit back our way with a huge grin. We all discovered that, apparently, Bo knows steamrollers, too, and he got the last laugh.

Bo was a great teammate to have around. I suspect the guys from the Kansas City Royals would say the same, as Bo's other job was playing Major League Baseball. Watching him with a glove or bat was just as awe-inspiring as observing him on the football field. During my post-season and his second season of the year, I had the opportunity to watch him play against the Angels in Anaheim.

After a couple of innings and a few too many beers, I worked my way down to the railing, squeezing into a mass of fans. I let out a crazy bellow like a bull moose that brought a smile to Bo's face as he ran over, instructing me to meet at the dugout after the game. I felt like the biggest cock on the block when I turned to walk back up to my seat. The fans in the vicinity must've wondered why Bo singled me out. Meanwhile, I spent the postgame in the locker room with his other sports family.

Talking Shop with Bo

For my sanity's sake, I needed friends outside of football to keep me balanced. If it had been all football, all the time, I would've burned out early in my career. While in-season, my teammates and I did almost everything together: practice, shower, eat, travel, bleed, and ache. I craved separation. I was fortunate to have a college teammate, Dave Gentzler, living a few houses away in Hermosa Beach. Most days, I would end up at his place after practice as I smelled his BBQ cooking up something delicious.

This was the perfect getaway from the intensity of ball and everything that came with it. When I hung out with my crew outside of football, we never discussed the game. I could park the aggression, and I never worried about someone thinking I was too soft. It was a relief to shed the macho tough shit and just be my authentic self.

The ability to learn and apply healthy psychological practices was a deciding factor in the longevity of my career. I knew too many guys that weren't so lucky. And I wouldn't see this side of them until it was too late. One of my dear Raiders teammates, loved by all, got drunk one night and died after he flipped his car. What pressures drove him to this end? We were all blindsided and crushed. Another fun-loving fourth-round picked teammate was cut after four seasons and blew his brains out. How could football be more important than his life? I would never get the chance to ask. A few others frequently got in bar fights, and still more took out their stresses on their girlfriends or wives.

The visible aftermath of domestic disturbance sauntered into the Cowboys' locker room one morning during my rookie year. As the team suited up for practice, the toughest son of a bitch veteran player walked in, grumbled good morning, and got dressed for practice like nothing was awry. Meanwhile, the rest of the team tried not to stare at his face. But like a car accident, no one could help themselves. I'm pretty sure my jaw was hitting the ground.

He finally narrowed his eyes and surveyed the room to be met with faces that immediately darted to the floor. If we had nothing to do, we busied ourselves in a hurry. No one dared say a word about the fingernail scratches that consumed his face. He would have to convince us that he was locked in a tiger's cage for it to make any sense. There were fresh scratches in every direction, some still bloody. Not wanting to get rag-dolled in front of the team, I didn't say a thing, but I was left wondering about his wife's condition. I hated seeing the slow but insidious corruption of our team's moral compass. And it was a poignant reminder that the pressure casualties were too many to count, which is all the more reason to establish and actively manage a healthy mindset. It's as essential as building those muscles.

While I always felt I had a solid mental and psychological composition, I fell off the proverbial horse a few times. The most regrettable instance occurred on a Monday evening when one of my Raiders teammates joined me for a high-dollar charity event. I broke out my favorite custom blue number that I saved for special occasions. After glad-handing and talking football, I took my final grin-and-grab lap around the gala to ensure I left everyone on a high note. Ready to chill over a beer, my teammate and I headed to a hotel sports bar for a more memorable night than anticipated.

As I took my first sip, this massive, athletic Samoan approached me, slurring insults. After years of experience, I was skilled at deescalating these testosterone tantrums. I diverted my eyes and offered my energy in other directions. But, without hesitation, he pressed into my personal space to taunt me. I flagged down a passing bouncer about half our size, but official, nonetheless. Feeling the rising intensity from my new acquaintance and the likely disturbance that would befall the general area, the bouncer demanded we step outside. I could immediately sense that this night was spiraling. So, my teammate and I headed for the door with the intention to keep moving and call it a night.

My large Samoan friend and his buddy had a different idea. But, as Mike Tyson wisely said, "Everyone has a plan until they get hit in the face." As I turned to leave, my new island mate blocked my path, spewed some ugly words, and, worst of all, spit on my favorite blue suit. While I felt fights were 99 percent avoidable, the odds quickly turned to that rare 1 percent.

Being forced into a fight was regrettable, but he escalated to this end. One of us was going to land the first punch. I wasn't dressed for a fight nor cared to be hit. So, I gave him a look away and brought everything I had in a tightly clenched fist. I connected with his nose, and he disappeared into the hedge. His pint-sized sidekick must've wanted to join him because, as quickly as he leaped at my teammate, he was airborne for the bushes too.

After sharing my dissatisfaction with the bouncer about his failure to defuse the situation, we split for the parking garage through the vast open-air lobby. It was eerily quiet, with a freshly buffed floor and a lone night clerk deep in paperwork. Just as I dropped my shoulders and finally relaxed, I turned to see our very bloody dance partners closing in to even the score. Since they would regret it the next minute, I firmly stated that I didn't want any part of this. I said it for everyone's benefit, but it fell on deaf ears. He pressed forward.

I offered him one last chance to end his thoughtless plan as I indicated where the next punch would land. Onward, he pushed, and the same clenched right bomb launched him until gravity could have its way, sending his limp body onto the marble floor. As I checked to make sure he was still conscious, I found him still muttering obscenities. Seeing him in this state hurt my soul and disturbed me for weeks.

Not long after this encounter, I learned the Samoan was driving home drunk and clocked a bicyclist with his car, killing him on the spot. Along with some relief to learn the guy was behind bars, I felt mixed emotions, including sadness, frustration, and even a surprising bit of empathy, as I wondered what life experiences led him down such a dark path.

I thought about my journey, recognizing that I was comfortable getting physical for my job, but I didn't want to deal with more of the same outside of football. This fight, along with hints from my mind and body, triggered thoughts of hanging up the helmet. I wanted to leave all the aggression behind.

Rumors started to surface suggesting the Raiders would move back to Oakland from Los Angeles, so I needed to do some more weighty introspection: Would I take this opportunity to retire and walk away from football? Was now really the right time? I was mentally tired of it, but physically, I had more gas in my tank. Ultimately, my side business, Cloudburst, captured my heart and gave me the closure I needed to pursue my passion as an entrepreneur.

As one would expect, Los Angeles shook the day I retired from football. It was January 17, 1994, the morning of the 6.7-magnitude Northridge earthquake. Small quakes weren't uncommon in Los Angeles, but this one jolted me to attention at 4:31 a.m. Glancing out my window, thirteen floors up, I watched two adjacent towers sway back and forth. *So that didn't just happen in the movies*, I noted as panic overtook my thoughts. The City Club towers were designed to roll if the quake was big enough, so clearly, it was formidable. I threw on whatever clothes and shoes were close, bolting for the front door as my oversized bathroom mirror exploded into the bedroom. My only goal was to get out before the aftershocks hit. By the time I got to the front door, it was jammed shut. I was trapped.

Grabbing the essentials, I shimmied out the kitchen window, landing on an open-air walkway below. As I scrambled toward the stairs, I heard my trapped neighbors clambering. I dropped my shoulder into their front door, blowing apart the metalwork. We all raced down the stairwell and scattered. My car was unscathed, so I slid in and sped away from towers and wires. I ended up at the Raiders' facility feeling numb. This was the original plan for the morning since I was announcing my retirement.

Everyone eventually straggled in with the same look of shock and awe, and for the first time that I can recall, no one was fined for being late. Hugs and slaps with all, I covered the gambit of feelings that morning. I was saying goodbye to brothers I had teamed with for years, but I was also shedding the heavy burden of sustained aggression. Walking out on the entrepreneurial plank, I was wise enough to stay positive, focusing on what was possible. It turned into a beautiful day, and lucky for me, the future looked bright.

My love affair with football lasted twenty-five beautiful years, more than most marriages, beginning with contact football at age ten and hanging up my cleats forever in 1994 at age thirty-five. While I matured considerably, as evidenced by my rapidly whitening hair, I had a front-row seat to the evolution of football. In the 1980s, when I started my career with the Cowboys, football was primal, and the rule book wasn't so thick. Quarterbacks would stand out there like raw meat to be mauled, and the offensive lines employed every grab-n-hold, trip, choke, and hit scheme to slow the defense down. Chronic traumatic encephalopathy (CTE) was unheard of in my early playing days. Careless, insensitive, and uneducated terms such as he "got his bell rung" or "took a nap" permeated the league as euphemisms for being knocked unconscious.

My one and only nap struck while I chased down an interception at the Coliseum. I was a bowling ball going for a strike as I dove headfirst into a convoy of linebackers. I was later told I had achieved my kamikaze mission, but that was long after waking up to see a startling blue sky and trainer Rod Martin bearing down on me.

"What day is it?" Rod demanded as his brow creased and eyes narrowed. "Do you know where you are, Doc?" He followed without a hint of sarcasm.

"I'm on a beach with a margarita," I said, just to screw with him. "It's Sunday in the Coliseum. Now help me up," I said as I worked to get my shit together. I hated this attention and wanted to get off the field as quickly as possible. I got to my feet fast but stumbled as my legs were the last to wake up. Todd Sperber, always my favorite trainer, joined us on the field to guide me toward the bench. These two guys had their hands full with 300 pounds of clumsy meat as we weaved our way off the field.

Since there was no concussion protocol in those days, I must've passed muster because I knew where I was. So, they cracked an ammonia cap for me to freshen up. It snapped my head back and blew my tear ducts open within an instant. Those caps could raise the dead. At least that was true for most players. On the next play, one of our wickedly tough defensive backs, Ronnie Lott, dove in to assist on a tackle. After the whistle, he was motionless until his body began to convulse. That was another sight that I never got used to. But the trainers collected the damaged goods and parked Ronnie next to me like another broken toy. They offered him a cap that rested on his upper lip as he inhaled several times harder than usual. Just watching those strong pulls, my head would jerk back, yet he didn't even flinch. Instead, the next referee whistle alerted him like a well-trained dog as Ronnie shook loose and retook his spot. Meanwhile, I was still working to recover from my hit as I looked on in shock.

Recovery Time

Since that was the only time I was knocked out in eleven years, I count myself among the lucky ones, as Bill Dwyre suggested in the *Los Angeles Times*. However, it concerns me that the league played naïve for so long. Any other business would've prioritized product safety and longevity. It was clear that my well-being wasn't their primary concern. Like livestock, I needed to produce because, as the Cowboys' Tex Schramm coldly stated, "The players are like cattle and the owners are ranchers. And the owners can always get more cattle."

It disappoints me to see Schramm's old-school mentality still alive and well as injured players are easily discarded for fresh meat. Moreover, the current concussion protocol needs a radical overhaul to avoid being out of touch with the medical community. As neuroscientist and professor of neurobiology at Stanford University School of Medicine Dr. Andrew Huberman explains, "There's no way to determine all the consequences of a head hit in the minutes and hours that follow. Safe to play is something that needs days to monitor to decide accurately." Not to mention the absence of medical equipment, MRIs, and the like, which are necessary for a comprehensive evaluation. I would bet that these assessment tools never make their way into locker rooms . . . too expensive, just get more cattle.

Every year guarantees another reminder of the flawed protocol. During the 2022 season, Miami quarterback Tua Tagovailoa was back on the field shortly after he absorbed a shocking blow to the head that left him staggering and grabbing for something only he saw. It made me ill watching this elite athlete in a moment of desperation. Apparently, the franchise-paid doctor and trainers cleared him, and he was back in play. Any rational person would question the staff's impartiality, given the source of their paychecks. Isn't this a fundamental conflict of interest? Yet, the porous approach and biased decision-making persist.

The increased risk of CTE is among the many reasons retired players fight to gain better health care and services from the NFL through our collective bargaining agreement. While the league benefited from our sacrifices on the field, they don't always hold up their end of the implied agreement once we're no longer useful to them.

I recall watching a *National Geographic* special on giraffes with my wife who paused the show during a particularly brutal fight scene. These giraffes lit into each other using their necks to generate momentum as they propelled their small heads into their opponents.

"What other animal uses its head as a weapon?" she asked.

I just smiled, paused, and pointed to my noggin.

At that moment, the gravity of CTE set in for my new wife. I could see the look of concern wash over her face. To put us both at ease, I've run through every brain scan and analysis offered to retired players.

My philosophy is to stay vigilant about my health and not bank on better services through the NFL since they've only ever offered crumbs. As the saying goes, if you're healthy, you have many problems. But if you're sick, you have one. If I can prevent the need for services down the line, I avoid the feelings of disappointment and abandonment I hear far too often from former players.

It's also my belief that improvements to equipment would better protect active players and prevent long-term damage that much of my generation now manage with varying degrees of success. Plus, better equipment would allow the league to promote the big hits players are bred to deliver. I believe bigger, stronger, and faster should be utilized, not handicapped by rule changes.

A Little Misunderstanding

If answering honestly, most football viewers admit to enjoying the violent hits but never want to see their favorite players injured. Since 2002, the NFL has made over fifty rule changes to eliminate dangerous tactics and reduce the risk of injuries, but these efforts slowed the game. While games average three hours and twelve minutes, there are only eleven minutes of true action... and don't get me started on the hundred commercials—pure insanity.

Meanwhile, in an average year,

68 percent of players suffer injury. Safer equipment thoughts screamed to get out of my head as my entrepreneurial instincts fired. I put pen to paper to develop a proposal for the evolution of NFL equipment. Think *Terminator* meets *Gladiator* but with real and available technology, not science fiction. I did my research, hired a designer, and laid out my vision *Jerry McGuire* style. I was on a mission with firm conviction and the science to back it up. I shared my proposal with the NFL, NFL Players Association, and various local chapters but only got a few polite responses. The league and players were just not ready. Not then, not now.

Bottom line, the sport is inherently violent. But there are plenty of other professions, equally dangerous, that have made vast upgrades and additions to their gear. Hockey, motocross, and even the military aggressively improved their equipment to better protect their resources. Why not football? Sure, helmet and shoulder pad materials have modestly advanced over the years. But if you look at the equipment from the 1970s and compare it to today's gear, it's sorely lacking in substantial improvements.

It's also hard to watch 330-pound athletes get tangled up in a mosh pit of mayhem with bodies flying, yet only a handful of knee braces are donned for protection. Almost every game, a player is assisted off the field because of a leg injury: knee, ankle, hamstring... you name it. Why aren't knee braces required for interior offensive and defensive linemen? Everyone would win—the fans, player, teammates, coaches, owner, family—and his bank account would be safer, too.

Meanwhile, I'm no engineer, but I believe there are ways to connect the helmet to the shoulder pads while still providing full mobility, with the pads helping to absorb blows to the head. This would reduce the chances of violent head snaps that rattle the brain and cause long-term damage. Then there's heat stress, not often talked about, but it also negatively impacts player performance and leads to fatigue, cramping, and a host of injuries. Where are the cool vests or suits to help alleviate this risk? My desire is to see better protection for the players and to reduce the penalties so a fundamentally violent game can be enjoyed.

It saddens me to think it may take more severe injuries or deaths for player safety to earn the attention it deserves. In the meantime, I'll continue to share my message with those who will listen. I maintain my steadfast conviction that changing football for the better is possible.

The annual Raiders reunions further reinforce my safety convictions as I see the avoidable long-term effects of a high-impact sport. We always spend some time talking over our aches and pains, but eventually, it's overshadowed by the laughter and love shared among the old warriors. Most of us are grateful to be healthy enough to come each year and enjoy each other. But for those who stop coming, we are left to wonder if the years of battling took their toll. We may never know.

The "once a Raider, always a Raider" team motto offers every guy who wore the jersey unrivaled treatment and respect from this franchise. Al Davis and his son Mark, the current owner, genuinely care for all who bled for them, quietly paying for medical bills, throwing fantastic events, and simply doing right by their guys with plenty of perks. At least among the teams I played for, the Raiders are remarkable in this regard. To top it off, they cover our expenses each year while providing valued space to reconnect. It's first-class all the way, from Napa wineries to suite parties and preseason games. Many of the earlier generations I loved to watch also show up: guys like Dave Casper, Fred Biletnikoff, Lester Hayes, and Ted "The Stork" Hendricks.

Each time I make the trek, I'm reminded of how special it is to be a part of this legendary brotherhood. While there are plenty of Raiderisms and assorted macho sayings, there's a distinct value system that runs back to the roots of the franchise. The owner was a self-made man who dreamed of bringing football to the working town of Oakland. The original Raiders, first named the Señors, played on an atrocious field, making little money. They were met with an abundance of critics who doubted the team's viability. Yet the owner, coach, and players shared a progressive vision.

They pulled up their bootstraps and sought the inclusion of all walks of life. In fact, they were among the first to recruit aggressively at Black colleges. My head coach, Art Shell, was another example of the forward-leaning Raiders. He was the first Black head coach in the modern era after working his way up the ladder as an outstanding player, then my offensive line coach, and ultimately the man calling all the shots.

Then the franchise, true to its core ethos, defied the prevailing norms again with a brilliant move to Las Vegas. The city and team are like long-lost brothers, meant to be rebels in arms. The gleaming Allegiant Stadium is a testament to the bond solidified between these parties. Honestly, I can't think of a better place for the Raiders to call home, and I am quite certain that Al Davis is looking down with a shit-eating grin.

This move was a long time coming after Al's frustrated game of hopscotch between Oakland and Los Angeles on a quest to secure skyboxes and other high-revenue-generating features that were promised but never delivered. Forever the league's pariah because of his defiance, Al eventually gave them the one-finger salute when he sued the league for the right to move the franchise. No matter the steep obstacles, he innately understood what was best for his organization. And throughout it all, his fondness for Las Vegas remained a constant. In fact, it was not unusual for him to camp out at his rumored suite in the city. Knowing Al and his grand visions, I suspect that's when he hatched the long-term plan to make Las Vegas home.

Al and Mark made us all proud, and we honor them, just as they honor us, at the annual reunions. Over the years, long after players hung up their cleats and coaches retired, hundreds still cleared their calendars for reunions. They wouldn't miss an opportunity to honor and reinforce the alchemy of this community. At the last several reunions, a few teammates and our wives slipped away for a decadent Cakebread wine tasting followed by a special evening with the full array of warriors who made the pilgrimage that year. All dressed to impress and pleasantly tipsy, we boarded the luxury bus and made our way into the immaculately groomed hills overlooking Napa Valley. As we entered a sprawling estate, the sun shimmered down on a hillside of lush vines. It was a view straight out of *Wine Spectator*. The estate was spectacular. As we departed the bus, we were greeted with glasses of champagne and finely appointed servers with trays of appetizers. They mingled among the guests along with photographers capturing the delight of old players reconnecting and sharing laughter, sometimes even buckling over as we recalled memorable knee slappers.

As the sun set in the distance, over one hundred former players and their guests were guided to trellis-covered reception tables for the climax of the evening. We feasted on steak and crab legs along with free-flowing wine for the next two hours. The stories continued to permeate the air along with toasts, more fits of laughter, and back slaps. If ever there was a color that represented joy, I could see it in the dusk sky that evening.

CHAPTER 6

TIME TO GROW

My buddy and I had a big Saturday night at Vertigo in downtown Los Angeles when I hit it off with this smoking-hot Playboy Playmate, Sydney. We got along so well that she asked me to be her date for the fabled New Year's Eve party at the Playboy Mansion. I'm pretty sure any red-blooded guy would've jumped at this opportunity. And I was never one to turn down a good time.

Attempting to keep it classy for the big event, I ordered a limousine, put on my custom tux, picked up a bouquet, and headed into Los Angeles to grab Sydney. She was looking sexy in a tiny red dress, or was it a nighty? Our night was off to a great start.

After confirming our names at the Playboy Mansion gates, the hostess voiced her approval of my fine tux. "But," she said coyly, "this is a pajama party.... We'll need to find you a robe."

"Do you have anything nice in an XXXL along with a pair of size-sixteen slippers?" I asked, already guessing the answer.

With a faint giggle, she handed me a paper-thin beige robe.

"No size-sixteen slippers, but if your feet are that big, you'll do just fine around here," she said with a smirk and wink directed at my date.

First, I hit the men's room to disassemble my kickin' tux and don this nasty robe straight out of *Gomorrah*. While I was in the bathroom the size of a small closet, a well-known celebrity busted in to do a line of coke, checking his plush robe in the mirror. I came out feeling quite self-conscious with the robe looking like a mini dress and the sleeves stretched tight around my beefy forearms. I took in the scene, quite a far cry from my Midwest roots. There were guys in outfits with matching slippers and cigars, all acting as if this scene was perfectly normal. The women were fantasy-worthy and pulled out all the stops as if they were peeled from the pages of the only calendar that mattered beyond the Cowboys' cheerleader annual edition.

Midnight came and went with plenty of kisses all around. By one o'clock, Sydney insisted that we head to the club where we had met a few weeks back. By this time, I was getting pretty comfortable at the mansion, so leaving was at the bottom of my list. After a persistent pressure campaign, I gave in, and we headed to Vertigo. When we arrived, three of the doormen called out Sydney's name like old friends. So now I'm thinking, *What the hell, she's a regular?* I enjoyed the clubs quite a bit back then, but the regulars were a different breed.

"Follow me," she purred. "It's gonna be great. I want to introduce you to the manager."

The club was thumping, but she had me follow her down a dark, gritty staircase where a couple of large security men greeted her by name, opening a shady looking door. We stepped in, and it was at least 100 degrees in this stuffy den. Some guy was sitting behind the most enormous pile of cocaine I had ever seen. It felt like I had just stepped foot on the *Scarface* movie lot.

He offered us a line, but before he finished speaking, Sydney looked like Tony fucking Montana with a Hoover vacuum for a nose. My eyes bugged out; I excused myself and both physically and figuratively closed the door. Her boyfriend's name was Coke, and I was ready to move on. After about thirty minutes on the dance floor with a few friends also partying there, Sydney emerged from the deep. She cut a swath staggering through the packed dance floor, looking so disheveled with crazy cocaine eyes, half-naked with her dress hanging off and a bare breast lighting the way. As she approached, so did her security friends.

I looked at the whole scene and said, "That's it. I'm out of here. If you want a ride, meet me out front in five minutes." After waiting outside in the limousine for half an hour, I decided to leave her to her path. I never saw or spoke with Sydney again, but I always hoped that she was able to extract herself from that spiral-inducing lifestyle.

The distraction of girls and parties soon took a back seat as my son, Jake, came along rather unexpectedly. I heard about this kind of thing happening, but it never crossed my mind that a weekend of fun could result in something so life-altering. Jake's mom, Laurie, was a wholesome beauty in town with her girlfriend and meeting up with my teammate. We hopped around the bars and beach parties that peppered Hermosa Beach. I was living in a great spot on the sand and was in my groove with football. But I was also happily taking advantage of all the partying that came with beach life. The four of us spent most of the weekend together, and I obviously got to spend some quality time with Laurie. It was a great weekend, but it ended with a goodbye kiss with no expectation of seeing each other again soon. Then, a couple of months later, I got a call that hit me harder than a two-by-four.

"Steve, it's Laurie." Her voice offered a hint of hesitation.

"Hey, you in town?" I asked, looking forward to the potential of another fun weekend together.

"No, not exactly." Her voice indicated that there was something important to share. But the line went quiet for a few seconds as the unease started to mount.

"Steve, I'm pregnant," she forced out, followed by another lengthy silence. Things were no longer awkward; they were downright shocking.

Waiting for my jaw to reconnect and the faint feeling to pass, I stammered, "It's not mine, is it?"

To drive the point home, she repeated, "I'm pregnant . . . and it's yours." I could hear her feet as they paced along the floor on the other end of the line.

Another uncomfortable silence. "What?" I was trying to buy time because I could feel myself beginning to panic. I had no idea how to handle this conversation. For once, I was at a loss for words.

"I don't know what to say, Laurie," I responded with an overly calculated enunciation as if my next call might be to a lawyer. Out of all the shock and awe moments of my life, this was topping the list. I was used to working hard and getting everything I wanted out of life, but this wasn't part of my wish list. My mind went into self-preservation mode and forced the ugliest, most insulting, but necessary next question.

"You sure it's mine?" I spat out without regard for Laurie and what she was going through.

"Yeah, Steve, it's yours. I'm certain," she said without skipping a beat. The pacing stopped, and it sounded like she finally sat down due to the heaviness of this situation.

"Okay, I don't want to sound like an ass here. . . . I know it's way too late for that, but I need to know for sure. I'll get a paternity test lined up," I said, donning my best adult voice. *Was I trying to get out of it? Prove it wasn't mine?* All I could see were spots in my vision with a buzz in my ears. *Is this what a panic attack felt like?* I was full of questions with no answers that day. No matter how hard I tried to justify my behavior, I had to admit I handled the call like a complete ass.

After the test proved that I was Jake's father, I visited Pittsburgh to see my son and figure out how to be a dad during the peak of my football career. Even though it was an inglorious beginning to our relationship, I started to enjoy the little dude, and we connected in Los Angeles or Pittsburgh during the offseason. Visiting Pittsburgh to see Jake naturally brought me into many uncomfortable situations with Laurie's parents and ten—yes, ten—brothers and sisters. But things eased over the years as they started to view me as a decent guy. Honestly, given how things started, I couldn't blame them for assuming the worst. Eventually, I found myself looking forward to the visits to see Jake in his environment and connect with Laurie's parents as we sat on the front porch in the evenings. We had enjoyable discussions, and I never felt judged, just loved and accepted. It was pretty remarkable, given the circumstances. Out of all the women and families in the world who could've raised my son, I hit the jackpot with Laurie's family.

The only uncomfortable thorn was crossing paths with Laurie's boyfriend, Dan, who was part of the picture well before her trip to California. He stayed with Laurie through the birth of my son and my many visits and trips after they married. I felt like the blockhead football player from the West Coast. It was hard to imagine being in Dan's shoes. That said, he genuinely cared for my son, treated him well, and raised a solid family with Laurie long after their world was upended. Dan was rock-solid, and I was grateful.

Despite all the strangeness before Jake's arrival on the scene, I covet the memories of my time with him. I remember having him in the locker room before kickoff when we played the Steelers in Pittsburgh one Sunday afternoon. It was so much fun having him join us on the turf for our pregame warm-up, but it was also distracting. I lost control of him running all over the place, yet team owner Al Davis sure spotted him, shouting, "Get that fucking kid off the field!" It was quite a scene to watch this six-year-old escaping capture and cutting through drills without a care in the world. If you have seen a puppy doing hot laps, running in circles, that was Jake bolting as fast as his short little legs would take him until he slid into me like home base.

When Jake would fly out to stay with me during the offseason, he would be the first one exiting the plane, escorted by an attendant who released this mini-me into my custody. Then it was game on with me turning into his shadow. Jake's job was to lead us out of the airport. He loved the game and the challenge of reading the signs as I followed close behind with the occasional hint. We played this game in restaurants, too, but then added further complexity when Jake would determine what we owed from a pile of cash on the table.

We would also go grocery shopping together so I could learn the foods he liked and teach him how to compare nutrition and cost. We made everything fun. Seeing the world through his joyful eyes was intoxicating.

Father and Son

Jake is my twin, with curly dark locks, a lot of scruff, and my frame. He has a heightened sensitivity to the world around him. Despite the imposing football exterior, I was a sensitive kid, too. When we talk now, I'm left with admiration for the man he has become and the obstacles he's successfully navigated. The most challenging part of our adult connection has been knowing how and when to give him space. As I confide in other parents, I realize this is all too common and a natural evolution of parent-child relationships.

In many ways, my love for Jake opened my heart to love more than just my family and football. I vowed to wait until my NFL career ended to consider marriage. Sure, I had plenty of girlfriends over the years, but I resisted diving in deeper out of fear of distraction. And if I'm really honest, I just wasn't ready. As it turns out, it took forty years before I made that commitment. Perhaps I was a bit naïve, but when I walked down that aisle, I intended to keep my eyes facing my wife and commit for life.

I have several people and experiences to thank for never cracking the door of marital infidelity. Growing up, my parents demonstrated an impeccable model to emulate through their display of deep love and devotion. Each night, when Dad arrived home after a long day, he only wanted a large scotch and water, his wife, and an uninterrupted hour to focus on her alone. We gave them their space, but I wondered many times from afar, *How do they have so much to talk about?* They chatted nonstop, laughed, and snuggled while enjoying their nightly cocktail. I learned about true dedication to a partner through their actions, not their words. I believe these observations watered my soul and influenced my decision to wait until I could fully commit to my wife.

As if my parents weren't reinforcing enough, I had a prestigious Cowboy to thank for driving the point home in my early twenties. When I arrived at training camp, I heard all the stories of what to expect from aggressive girls to friends I didn't know I had trying to influence me. Following our night meetings, many of us would race to El Torito to grab a couple of beers and mingle with the bevy of girls. Though this was flattering and fun for the younger guys, I observed some married players kissing, exchanging numbers, or coupling up with girls at the bar. While I respected them on the field, I viewed them as weak for breaking their vows. Then there was Doug Cosbie, our good-looking tight end who wore himself out pushing girls back. He was always waving his wedding ring and begging for help to get the girls away. I wanted to be a Doug Cosbie. His strong morals and behavior were fixed in my mind for the remainder of my career.

When the universe deemed me ready and worthy, I met my first wife, Monique. As she opened the door to meet me for our blind date, she shared later how shocked she was by my appearance. I was sporting a geeky outfit of white socks and white shoes with my button-down shirt tucked inside my shorts. Not exactly a former football player vibe. That said, it worked, but she forever reminded me how she hoped the inside was better than the wrapping.

While our connection was amazing, we both had baggage. Monique lost her husband in a tragic accident a few years earlier. As for me, I didn't have the best track record when it came to monogamy. And I was selfishly concerned about getting tangled up with a girl fifty miles down the 405 freeway, one of the busiest highways on the planet. Nonetheless, love prevailed, and to this day, I don't regret one minute of my time with Monique.

I grew in ways I couldn't predict during our decade together. After years of keeping things surface-level in relationships, she guided me on a path toward greater emotional understanding and expression. With her, talking about feelings and working to deconstruct their true meaning was okay. Therapy was acceptable, if not encouraged, and considered a valued component of overall wellness. This was a refreshing change and the start of a new period of growth.

This phase didn't come without its set of challenges, however. If I was going to commit to a new life in Orange County, it was time to sell my business, Cloudburst (more on that venture later). The one-hundred-mile commute between my new home and Cloudburst headquarters in Simi Valley was untenable. So, my partner, Mike Davis, and I shook hands on a deal and closed it fast. This turned out to be a wise decision. It freed me up to dive into my new life. Meanwhile, Monique indulged her interest in real estate, building luxury homes best suited for magazine covers.

Monique's world was large and increasingly complex, and my life was growing perfectly uncomplicated as I cleaned up loose ends in Los Angeles. Finally, after a year of dating, she sent an assistant to sift through my bachelor wares before our worlds could converge. I was so in love that I would've gone empty-handed and practically did.

I'll never forget my first Christmas as I settled into Monique's home and my new life. This was in Southern California, where Christmas is often expressed through light-adorned palm trees. Monique had a tradition that dropped my jaw. And I would bet I wasn't alone. To create the Christmas ambiance, she hired massive ice-eating snowblowers to propel snowflakes across the house and lawn: our very own Orange County snow globe. It was outlandishly excessive, but the reactions of the neighborhood kids were priceless. Even though I wanted to challenge the practicality of this tradition, I learned to keep my opinions to myself. This was her show, her rituals, and I was meant to complement this world, not disrupt it.

The feeling of unease was compounded by a visit to her offsite storage units after the holidays to return her Christmas paraphernalia. To my amazement, it was our mini-Home Depot. It included a warehouse wing housing an extra car, a boat, lawn furniture, living room sets, beds, seasonal kitchenware, and more holiday décor than Nordstroms. Seeing so much unused stuff and the excess of it all was a startling sign of the profound differences in our approach to life. While I was focused on need, Monique chose want, with plenty of space to store it all.

In hindsight, I recognized that moving down to Newport Beach took all neutrality out of the relationship. I felt like the new kid on the block as Monique and her first husband were a power couple in town. My new friends had well-established friendships with the couple. Though we loved each other madly, the balance was grossly off-kilter. She employed a well-oiled team left over from her first husband. Meanwhile, I was a gang of one plugging into her world.

Monique's last teardown purchase and three-year rebuild proved too much for our struggling marriage. Though we refrained from raising our voices, the rising tensions were bubbling over and about to affect those around us. A feisty older couple who lived next door began airing their complaints about construction trucks blocking their driveway while workers extended their hours beyond the city cutoff. But that was just one of the many complaints coming our way.

Once the neighbors threatened to call the city, I knew it was nearing game time and I had to pay the neighbors a visit. But before I could get out the door, she poked the bear several more times to stoke the rage. My darkness was near pregame level as I shot out the door with fists clenched, planning to punch my neighbor in the face when he opened the door.

As I stomped across our yard, huffing and puffing, I was hit with a cosmic jolt. I'm not a religious guy, but I was physically stopped in my tracks as tears began flowing down my face. My shoulders relaxed, my fists released, and all I could think was *What the hell am I doing?* I stood there for a few moments, trying to absorb this unexpected mindset reversal. I felt myself let go of the darkness. After gathering my wits, I continued to my neighbor's doorstep in the most humbled state.

I simply asked him to dump all his aggression on me. I was there to listen. He was taken aback and shared many issues from a safe distance, but he realized my intent was sincere as he shared his appreciation for my visit. Monique was waiting at the door upon my return, fully expecting to see blood from a fight. Instead, from that day forward, our neighborly relationship was an open and easy channel of communication. I wish I could say the same for my marriage, but it wasn't meant to be.

It was incredibly painful to love someone so much but not have the ability to make it work. No amount of couples therapy nor introspection could guide us through the maze of dissimilarities we encountered over ten years of marriage. I learned the hard lesson that sometimes love really isn't enough. Even with that revelation, the last year of our marriage was an on-again, off-again rollercoaster of emotional exhaustion. Nonetheless, my love for her remained constant.

I had no interest in dating for a long time after my divorce. I was hurt, and any savoir faire I possessed previously, which was little to none, was long gone. I remember being in the baking aisle at the grocery store when a looker approached me making small talk.

"I haven't seen you here before," she said with a warm smile as she ran her fingers through her ponytail and adjusted her top.

"Yeah, I'm just picking up some stuff on my way back from the gym." I was caught red-handed with a cylinder of cookies that I dropped to my side out of view. As much as I worked out and ate right, I was a sucker for chocolate chip cookies.

"You don't look like you eat those," she said as she pointed to my arm, tossed her head back, and angled her hips closer to me.

I was immune to her advances and stepped right into the confessional instead. "Yeah, it's a bad habit," I blurted out, shifting my weight and lowering my gaze. Wow, I was nervous. *What the hell was going on? Where was the Doc from my playing days?* The ensuing silence was deafening.

Finally, she cocked her head, and I watched a befuddled look wash over her face as her well-plumped lips contorted. "Alrighty then, guess I'll see ya around," she said, flashing a phony smile. She reached for her cart, motioning to the next aisle. Obviously, she couldn't wait to escape this socially awkward leper.

Now I was far more embarrassed about my lack of game than my cookie addiction. I couldn't believe my discomfort and inability to flirt. In some strange way, I felt beholden to my wedding vows to Monique even though our marriage was in the rearview mirror. I put the cookies down, left the store, and headed to the self-help section of Barnes & Noble next door to dive deeper into myself.

I spent the next two years in my own little world, focused on introspection and growth. Most mornings, I rose early and ran on the beach as the sun lifted out of the sea. I left my headphones at home and would purposely listen to the stillness to find peace and stay in tune with the universe. I returned from these runs on a natural high, trusting that I was right where I needed to be. My positive mindset had flickered during the last years of my marriage. However, the universe was now subtly reminding me that anything was still possible with the right attitude and outlook.

I explored every nook and cranny of my heart and mind over this monk-like period of solitude. By the close of the second year, I was coming out of my hibernation and itching to get back into the world around me. I felt the low hum of the universe, and I took it as a sign that I had done the work to heal. I also started to feel like I was treading water in Huntington Beach, not in a bad way, but I was getting too comfortable in my routine. At this rate, I would be the cookie-consuming dough boy biking through town.

I knew I needed to mix things up, so I timidly dipped my foot into the online dating world. I had zero expectations. I assumed it would be a source of entertainment and maybe a few fun dates to disrupt my usual patterns of the beach, bike rides, gym, and baking aisle. It helped that I expected little. The first few dates were total disasters, followed by an emotional basket case who broke up with me by shipping smashed framed pictures; I kid you not. I was beginning to doubt the quality of the algorithms when they spat out a suggested match that caught my eye. I devoured her profile. She fit the stereotype of a Manhattan Beach girl: tall, blond, and sporty, but there was far more to the equation, which I sensed within minutes.

I came to understand, in time, that she was the yin to my yang. Lizzy and I don't line up well on paper by any stretch of the imagination, but we are strangely compatible. She's an East Coast girl at her core: driven, focused, and short on small talk. She holds degrees from Harvard and Georgetown with the résumé that would accompany this pedigree. She's athletic, but that was always secondary to cultivating her mind. We would've never met if she hadn't moved west to change the trajectory of her life. This was when I entered the equation.

We met a week after our online introduction, and our connection was electric. When I pulled into her neighborhood, she texted me, "Running behind, just come in, leaving the door unlocked." I took this as a sign that we built some trust over the phone. I decided to take the plunge, too, having faith that what I saw in her profile was about to come to life before my eyes. I was all hope as I drove down her street. My light and positivity had returned with renewed force, and I was about to be rewarded.

As I parked in front of her place, memories of my time living in the area, just a town south in Hermosa Beach, danced through my mind. This area was a true gem, and I often hit the bar at the top of her street during my playing days. It sat on the north end of town, known for its surf break, beach bars, and laid-back atmosphere. The houses on her street looked like an anthill of unkept beach shanties with no flashiness whatsoever. It was a place you would choose to live if your focus was the beach life. I already jibed with her priorities.

As I opened the warped and salt-crusted screen door, I heard the faint sound of a shower and the whine of a loose fixture rattling as the water stopped.

"Hey, it's Steve," I said to avoid being accused of being a voyeur in a stranger's home. This was definitely not treading water behavior.

I heard a faint mumble that I took as confirmation of my presence in her place. I sat down on the couch and looked out to the ocean but also kept an eye on the hallway in Christmas-like anticipation. When Lizzy appeared, she only wore a damp towel and a big smile. She confidently walked over to me, wrapped both arms around my neck, and planted a warm, wet kiss that will forever make my top-ten memories. We finally broke loose and stared for a moment, followed by unmistakable knowing smiles. We didn't make it to our dinner reservation that night, which was exactly how it was supposed to be. I met a woman who was entirely different from me, but I was ready to burn the boats. I was all in. Two months later, I put my house up for lease and joined Lizzy on the next chapter of my journey back to my old stomping grounds, but a wiser and better man.

If I had met Lizzy at any other time in my life, I'm confident that it wouldn't have worked, which reminds me that there's a time and place for everything. There are a couple of reasons: If I had met her during my Dallas days, she would've been a number. During the tail end of my career, the East and West Coast divide would've reduced us to a fling. Next, I was so focused on Cloudburst and then Monique that we would've passed each other without a second glance. And if I'd never met Monique and explored the depths of my emotional being, Lizzy would've rejected me outright, as she had little interest in superficial players.

Lizzy is a modern-day Spartan who shows no interest in things. She has this extreme aversion to stuff, preferring white walls and empty space. We harmonize in our dislikes and have a saying we use with each other often that I practiced but never preached for the last decade: is that a need or a want? This helps us stay the course and lighten our footprint. This wasn't part of a quest to support climate change or something that noble. It was born out of a desire to keep life as simple and streamlined as possible. Without distractions, our commitments are few, and our minds run free.

We are real-deal minimalists. When people enter our place for the first time, I witness a flicker of surprise. Even though we live in one of the global epicenters of consumerism, there's no dining table to clutter up our space, no television to waste our time; there's just a single cozy chair for each of us to enjoy the evenings. It would feel strange to many, but our living room houses our surfboards and a massage table while a bench and weights fill out our dining space. Each item is essential and used daily. And no, I don't get massages each day. I use it to stretch every morning and evening as part of my warm-up and cooldown. I would recommend that every couple get a massage table for other reasons, too, but that topic is for another kind of book.

I wasn't keen on marrying again, and nor was Lizzy. We each had traditional marriages under our belts and no desire to replicate those experiences. But there was something about the depth of our connection that told us this would last for the rest of this ride on Earth. So, it was a relatively quick conversation that led to our nuptials.

We were lying in the sand on Manhattan Beach on a lazy Sunday afternoon when Lizzy rolled over and commented, "We should probably just get married," in the same tone that one would indicate the need to put ketchup on the grocery list. This was her East Coast practical side in its full glory.

I paused, then smiled, mimicking her tone and affect. "Sure, why not?"

"No, seriously, getting married on a deserted beach seems

fitting," she said. "And we must be naked." I've never met someone who has such a dislike for clothing. Yes, minimalism permeates all aspects of this woman.

I pulled out my phone to draft a quick note to our buddy who enjoyed the winter months on his sailboat in the Caribbean. We joined him once before, and it was the most laid-back adventure. By day, we would chart our path to a different island, spend time mingling with the locals in town, and in the evenings, we would lounge in the cockpit while discussing world affairs, life, and, of course, the stock market since Tom was a financial guru who traded in his successful practice for the good life. He was just the perfect amount of chill to be both our boat captain and wedding officiant. Plus, he was open-minded enough to marry us naked without a second thought. In fact, he was dressed down a bit from the pastor for my first wedding. He was sporting only his underwear, hat, and sunglasses when we made our commitment.

It all went down in March 2014, six months later. It was supposed to be on March 17th, but we showed up at the deserted island, Mopion, in the Grenadines, and the swelling clouds started to converge and swallow up the beautiful blue sky.

"Hey, Tom," I said. "Wanna come back tomorrow and marry us then?"

"Perfect, let's grab some pizza on Petit Saint Vincent. I need a break from peanuts," he said without hesitation, preparing to tack.

So that night, we feasted on fresh Caribbean pies and a few Caribs, a local beer from Trinidad and Tobago. As we were walking back to the dock, I pointed out a lush flowering tree. Lizzy didn't plan on carrying a bouquet or anything of the sort, so I tore off a branch.

"For the minimalist." I bowed, handing the shop-worthy bouquet to Lizzy.

"These will go great with my dress," she said sarcastically.

The following day, we woke early and crossed the bay again to our low-key wedding venue. This day was textbook perfect. The sky was crystal blue with a few high wisps and a light warm wind. We elected to take the dinghy to the island because a bull shark was known to monitor the reef perimeter during feeding times, and it was nearly breakfast. I was fine with pressing our luck after the wedding with a swim, but there was no need to ruin a good thing before it started.

The wedding was raw, perfect, and yes, completely nude. Lizzy even managed to get me to shed tears with her vows:

> *Why do I want to marry you?*
>
> *Because, in the first moments of the day, you make me smile, and in the last moments of the night, I feel safer and more loved than I have ever known.*
>
> *Because you make me a better person, more compassionate and patient than I am on my own.*
>
> *Because I feel fully alive when we are together. I carry security about the safe space we always return to, knowing that this is worth protecting.*
>
> *Because I want the world to understand what you mean to me and how anything before was just a part of the path to you.*
>
> *Because something this good, and this effortless, comes along just once . . . if we are lucky.*
>
> *What do I pledge to you? When I look at you twenty years from now, my mind will still see this gorgeous body because your soul is just as beautiful.*
>
> *I will put my life vest on first, but you will be next.*
>
> *I will honor you, Love, forever. And express my connection to you with tremendous pride, always. I am blessed beyond words to spend the rest of my life with you.*

I would love to share my vows, too, but they took flight in the trade winds and probably gave someone on a nearby island a smile that day.

We celebrated our commitment without worrying about the caterer, guest list, size of the cake, or any other things that could tarnish the purity of the experience. Both of us were fully present in our birthday suits, honoring what we created and blessing what would come. Then we plunged into the water and swam back to the sailboat, bull shark be damned.

Dressing Up for the Camera

I never professed to have a type nor believed in soulmates, but it all flows so easily when it's the right person at the right time. I can count on one hand the number of times we raised our voices. And we instinctively defer to each other's strengths. I'm the go-to guy when addressing issues with neighbors or mingling in a crowd. However, if it requires planning and detail, like travel, I put all my chips on Lizzy every time.

Not all is perfect, though; there's one blind spot we possess that can get us into trouble. We are both risk-takers and like moving fast. I heard about a property on the Big Island of Hawaii that my old buddy was looking to sell fast. We cleared our calendars for the next morning without hesitating, and I grabbed our flights. We rallied so fast that we neglected to examine a map closely. As our flight descended to the island, the pilot came onto the intercom to address the particulars of the weather on the ground and transfer gates. But what caught my attention was the name of the town where we were landing. I had booked the wrong flight. We were headed into Kona instead of Hilo.

"Holy crap. Wrong airport," I admitted.

Lizzy gave me a big smile and just laughed. "Guess it's time for some fun," she said as her bean started running the traps on all the changes needed to get from Kona to Hilo.

As it turns out, we landed four hours away from Shangri-La, having to cross a volcano to get there. It turned into quite an adventure that we capped off with a day at a nude beach followed by a rave party. It was a good thing that we decided against the impulsive purchase. Three years later, Kilauea lava enveloped the property. All was lost.

Ironically, the most significant conflict we experienced in our marriage was outside our bond. Sure, I heard the warnings about mixing family and business, but like many others before me, I naïvely believed that my solid, happy-go-lucky family was different. My Wright lineage goes back to the early 1500s when John Wright sat in the House of Lords under King Henry VIII. Yet, no matter the lofty heritage or high-minded ideals, it didn't take long for this volatile experiment to leave many relationships in tatters. It was anything but happy-go-lucky and a certain embarrassment to any king's court.

It all started before my generation of Wrights entered the picture. Like his grandfather before him, Dad and his brother were gifted six hundred acres of Iowa farmland, dating back to the 1850s. When my generation eventually entered the picture, we explored joint development of the property that showed great promise, or so I hoped.

Over the years, different family members attempted to lead the circus, but eventually, it got too ugly with Dad and his brother threatening to sue one another. But that was only a foreshadowing of things to come. Finally, the two brothers quelled the feud by dividing the land. It took about five years to patch the frayed relationship, but some damage was irreparable.

After the land was divided, my generation attempted a similar play at developing our half of the property, only to end in precisely the same spot with the land dissected even further. The effort was doomed due to unchecked egos and miscommunication from all sides. I remember endless nights of heated phone calls followed by venting to Lizzy. She eventually had enough of the aggressive and corrosive energy clouding our sanctuary. While the missed opportunity and disconnect among siblings ate me up, my wife retreated from a family in shambles. It was clear what needed to happen. I'd get out and focus on the most important things: my sanity and relationship with my love.

I can count on one hand the number of times I've seen this woman cry, and over half of those were due to my family stress along with the high intensity that comes from working in the investment world. As it turned out, during a lengthy family call, Lizzy hatched a new plan. "I think we should travel the world."

The next day, she persisted with renewed vigor. "I'm serious. Let's really do this. Why not?" Lizzy asked aloud as she thought through the implications.

I could think of a million trivial reasons why not, but one huge reason to go: for an experience of a lifetime. Along with grabbing life and shaking it, we would get some much-needed space from a tough family situation and free my caged bird from her life in the corporate world. It was time for Lizzy to rediscover her song.

By the end of the following weekend, we established a general route that took us through the South Pacific from Fiji, Samoa, Tonga, and New Zealand to Australia, Indonesia, Singapore, Sri Lanka, the Maldives, and France. Next, we were headed to Latin America to wander through Brazil and Peru. Our final stop was in Costa Rica for a month before heading back Stateside to Miami. No one I know digs into a project like Lizzy. Once we had a rough route, she spent her free weekends researching and managing the detailed planning like a second job. With this job, however, I could hear her song returning and smiled at the imminent opening of the cage door.

Lizzy calculated her exit from the investment world, and we moved into downtown Los Angeles while she finished out the last six months of work. In many ways, the trip started at this point. It felt like foreign travel to leave the beach and move into a high-rise in the heart of downtown. You can't live in Los Angeles County and not know about the homeless problem, but to know and experience it are entirely different. One morning, I received an early insight when accompanying Lizzy on the seven-block walk from our condo to her work. We were talking about destinations in Sri Lanka when Lizzy pulled back and froze.

"Geez, this place is tragic," she said as she motioned with her eyes.

I followed the direction of her gaze to a man sprawled out on the sidewalk with his pants down, masturbating in full sight, who was offering guttural groans as his body gyrated. "What a huge bummer," I commented, shaking my head in amazement.

Just then, a city bus pulled up, and commuters flooded off with looks of disgust on their faces. There was nothing to be done but to keep moving and divert our eyes.

Then we discovered that traffic sounds weren't the most significant concern in this city. After about three nights, we learned that it was nearly impossible to mute the shouting from the street below. In most cases, mental illness was at play with nonsensical yelling. It was difficult to hear but even more distressing to watch. Homeless people need real help, not spare change. In Los Angeles County, the magnitude of the problem is staggering, with over 75,000 homeless. It's virtually a city of people lacking services. We grew accustomed to the noise, but never with the disregard these people experienced.

Once Lizzy pulled the rip cord at work, Habitat for Humanity helped us empty our condo. It was liberating to part ways with what little we had left after years of embracing minimalism. One of the last things to go was football memorabilia after taking plenty of photos to save in the cloud. This turned into quite a reflective and humbling exercise to toss cherished pieces right along with old kitchen towels and red solo cups. I remember placing my plaques, awards, and football gear into large boxes and positioning them in the corner of the room, like a waiting area for my memories. By the end of the week, I could no longer delay the inevitable.

Toting a container at a time, I made my way through the alley to the nearest dumpster and released each box into the abyss. I'll never forget looking down in the open filth after the last box was emptied and seeing the Ed Block Courage award trophy nestled into some dirty diapers. After I closed the lid and started to walk away, I had to run back for one last look. Every year, the thirty-two franchises in the NFL vote for one member of their team who, in their eyes, "exemplifies commitment to the principles of sportsmanship and courage." This was an honor that now the dumpster could enjoy. It was part of my memory, which would have to be enough.

By the end of the pretravel purging process, we had four of everything essential in the kitchen and a slimmed-down wardrobe. In addition to lightening our load through donations, we went entirely paperless with all our essential documents in the cloud instead of piled up on our desks. It wasn't the easiest process, but I never looked back once I went down the minimalist path. I found that if you can stay disciplined and resist the urge to add nonessentials, the freedom and lightness you receive are valuable gifts.

Just before we left, we made a last-minute decision to store our surf gear at a buddy's property in Malibu. Little did we know that only two months later, one of the worst fires in Malibu's history would rip through his world along with the properties of so many other residents. We were among the lucky ones to lose so little and avoid the devastation.

Once our remaining car was loaded with the consolidation of our world, we boarded a plane, knowing that we wouldn't be back on US soil for a year. During our time abroad, we stayed in thirteen different countries and slept in forty-five different beds, many of which were backbreakers but a place to rest our heads. As we planned, our first stop was to Samoa and then Tonga to receive shipments of sports equipment for Globall Giving and deliver them to local schools with our Peace Corps partners.

We could feel the internal decompression begin as we went from the pace of downtown Los Angeles to island time. Then our lungs thanked us as we replaced city smog and noise with thick tropical air and exotic birds. It was the people more than anything that made Samoa and Tonga special. As big and tough as some of these dudes were, if I shined my light and gave them a genuine smile, I would always get one in return.

Our first few nights brought us to Lalomanu, Samoa, where we were accepted by the locals. Meals at the beach fales, a collection of thatched huts, were family-style. So, we planned our time not to miss these communal events. As we dined together, we heard from locals who lost family and friends in the great tsunami of 2009 that hit the area with seventy-two-foot waves. They had such kindness in their hearts and were so generous with their time that it was impossible not to love them all. We wanted to help in some way, so we offered up our car for them to run errands, and this was quite a hit. Throughout the evenings and early mornings, we would get taps on the hut to run to an auntie's place or grab supplies from across the island. It offered plenty of entertainment, and I'm glad we could help them a bit.

Connecting in Samoa

I fell hard for this young bartender, Hemi, who wanted to get in shape for his girlfriend. He was in love and thought if he put on muscles, his girl would love him more. Oh, boy. I had my hands full with Hemi, who was quite obese. But I admired his big heart and fire. During our lengthy discussion, he admitted that he had never exercised in his life. I decided to go easy. Our first goal was to complete ten consecutive burpees, but he got to three and felt faint, so we rested. We talked about our plan for the next couple of days and finished our training, agreeing to meet at eight o'clock. The next morning, Hemi rolled in around eleven o'clock after Lizzy and I completed our training, ate breakfast, and swam. But remember, we were on island time. So instead of exercising, he wanted us to join him for a cold spaghetti sandwich lunch: a carbohydrate bonanza.

Hemi shared that he was so sore and worn out from our workout the day before that he couldn't manage to get up in time for our training. I figured there was no chance we would make any progress, but I couldn't help but love the kid. Since he felt so bad about missing that morning, he wanted to try again the next day. So, eight o'clock came and went. Lizzy and I finished our training. Then Hemi showed up around ten o'clock eating what looked like a loaf of bread ... no condiments, just a fricking loaf of bread. This island chill life was so attractive to me; there was no hurrying, and plans were always fluid.

We decided we would try one more time and agreed to meet for breakfast at nine o'clock. He arrived a few minutes early because it was Pancake Friday, and he loved cakes. So, we discussed life, enjoyed breakfast, and departed with fantastic memories of our Samoan friend, who demonstrated more island wisdom than I could've offered through training.

Our efforts to get sports equipment to the local schools helped us feel that we were providing something in return for our time in the islands. These projects were the brainchild of my buddy, Mark Rolison, a good Midwest guy with a huge heart for kids. The nonprofit Globall Giving operates under a simple yet powerful motto: all kids deserve a chance to play. To that end, we collect used sports equipment from families throughout the US to provide this gently used equipment to kids in need around the world. We've worked in over thirty countries and impacted over a million kids.

Globall Giving Donations, Tonga

Boards for the Groms in the Philippines

While our time in Samoa and Tonga filled our hearts, our stay in Sri Lanka proved to be the most impactful. We spent several weeks in the south, mainly in Hikkaduwa. While it was a naturally beautiful area, it wasn't without its dangers. In fact, it was the target of a terrorist bombing just two months after our departure.

During our stay, we focused on finding community centers and schools needing sports equipment. A tuk-tuk proved to be the best way to move about the area, with our driver darting in and out of the frenetic traffic while spiders and other enormous, unidentifiable critters hooked rides in our cabin. Did I mention my irrational fear of spiders? Yeah, I couldn't wait to get out of the tuk-tuk at each stop.

On one of our excursions, I noticed an imposing sign along the road, written in Sri Lanka's official language of Sinhala, but I was able to make out the word tsunami. I knew that a seismic sea wave had hit the southwest coast, but I had little knowledge beyond the basic facts. I motioned toward the large sign, and the driver nodded. My hand clutched the door handle as we jostled through the muddy potholes of the vacant parking lot. The place didn't look promising, but I was ready to bid farewell to the four-inch spider that took refuge on the ceiling of the tuk-tuk.

Given my size, exiting the tuk-tuk was always an adventure as I unfolded myself. Just as I managed to get fully upright, a young guy opened the front door and motioned for us to join him inside. As it turns out, this was the Community Tsunami Museum, and the man who greeted us ran the facility in honor of his family. The museum was filled with site maps and raw images from 2004 capturing the devastation that included over 30,000 deaths in the coastal area. There was no Western whitewashing of the photos. It was horrific. In many cases, entire families were destroyed by the massive waves that toppled homes and even flipped an ill-timed passenger train.

It was 2018, fourteen years had passed, but rebuilding efforts were slow, and services for families remained woefully inadequate. With the help of Google translator, I explained our nonprofit, and his eyes lit up as his body mimicked a volleyball serve. I must've looked puzzled because he checked Google translator as we passed the phone back and forth, entering sports terms. As it turns out, volleyball is the official sport of Sri Lanka. Meanwhile, back in Southern California, beach volleyball might as well be our defining sport, so I had easy access to the equipment these kids needed. This was the type of chance meeting that I sought during our travels. Because of that exchange, we were able to bring light and joy to an area in need.

We spent time in Rio de Janeiro on another leg of our journey. I wanted to experience this magnificent place with Lizzy. Thirty years prior, I came for Carnivàle with two teammates and partied for a week straight. I remember the easy living, free-flowing caipirinhas, gorgeous beaches, and mind-blowingly beautiful women. It was paradise.

As with almost all things in life, having expectations can be a fast-track to disappointment. I was shocked to see how much the area had changed. Life looked hard. I could see it on people's faces. Alcohol was overwhelmed with sugary mixers. The beaches were trash-ridden. The girl from Ipanema had vanished, and I was ready to move on after only a few days in the city.

The year of traveling gave us plenty of time to discover how to operate more efficiently and live comfortably with less. About two weeks into our time on the Samoan Island of Savai'i, we were annoyed with the process of washing our clothes in the small sink. Out of frustration, I wore my stuff into the outdoor shower and scrubbed away. It worked beautifully, and our showers became our nightly washing machine for the rest of the year.

We also got sick of carrying a duffel bag in addition to our carry-on backpacks. It was only half full of unused stuff, so we sent it home with a friend visiting Indonesia and never missed it. It was a breeze to navigate in and out of airports with just a carry-on. To make this manageable, I stuck to wearing the same three swim trunks and T-shirts in rotation, which suited Lizzy just fine as she was keeping to her sequence too. When we returned to the US, those items didn't even make the Goodwill donation bag; they were burned upon arrival.

We adopted a few standard travel tips from fellow vagabonds in Tonga. They suggested entering the phone numbers and addresses of local urgent care centers when arriving at a new destination. Given all the surfing we were doing, it made sense, and it's something that we've carried forward to all our travels. We also leaned on a few phone applications that made life a lot easier: Units Plus for quick conversions of all sorts, along with Google Translator, Uber, and Airbnb.

As the saying goes, you're a product of your environment, for better or worse. It would've been easy to stay in my little Malibu bubble with semiannual exotic getaways to gated resorts. But we deliberately focused on living like a local and interacting with everyone to learn, experience, and grow. From machete-wielding kids in the hills of Samoa to bank tellers in the cramped quarters of Malé and passionate soccer coaches in Nosara, the vast majority were welcoming and kind. While we are strangers by tongue or life path, we all seek the same thing: happiness. If you bring nothing else, go with your positive light leading the way and watch the world open up to you.

CHAPTER 7

OPPORTUNITY KNOCKS

My philosophy of charging through open doors was in full force when reality television first entered my world in 2009. I was on the set of *Fox NFL Sunday* to catch up with Howie and share a few laughs about our years as teammates. When he left to kick things off in the studio, I struck up a seemingly benign chat with a stranger in the green room. The brief encounter planted a seed that ultimately led to thirty-one days of mind-bending starvation on primetime television. I had no clue what awaited me when I joined the twenty-second season of *Survivor*.

While I feel fans deserve to hear more from contestants about what goes on behind the scenes, I would be eyeball-deep in legal trouble or hiding out in the Andes Mountains if I shared anything. So, like many contestants before and after me, I must refrain from discussing my experience on the southwest coast of Nicaragua, where time froze and my light grew dim.

Following my stint on reality television, I landed back in Los Angeles with my front tooth bothering me enough to make an emergency dentist

*After Survivor,
Down Thirty-One Pounds*

appointment. After an examination, the concerned doctor disappeared to look at the X-rays and informed me that he was pulling it out immediately. "Your current bacteria level kills people in Third World countries, Steve. You don't mess with this," he said.

So, out with my front tooth . . . welcome home. I was quite a sight, so I decided to lay low for a while since I looked like a walking skeleton with a distracting smile. At least this tooth issue stayed dormant until my return to civilization. I'm left wondering what it would've done to the ratings to have my tooth extracted by tribemates using handmade tools on television. I'm so thankful that it never came to pass.

While *Survivor* was tough, one of my most challenging experiences became a labor of love. I was enjoying an evening of margaritas at Las Casuelas in Palm Springs a couple of months before training camp in 1992 when I stumbled into entrepreneurship. It wasn't my intent, but like other things in my life, being open to possibilities ultimately led to the creation of my company, Cloudburst. I watched the continuous spray of mist that dusted patrons who seemed grateful for the cooling effect during a blistering heat wave in the desert. After learning the system's simplicity, I pieced one together and tried cooling the sideline for the Raiders first preseason game. Coach Shell was hesitant at first to try anything out of the norm. But I promised to remove it myself if he saw no value. As it turns out, Coach and my teammates loved it, so I knew I was onto something good after that first game.

The system also caught the attention of a few important suits in the stands who flagged down a ball boy to pass me their business cards. After the final whistle, still in full game attire, I had my first real business meeting about installing my system at the Hollywood Park racetrack. Keep in mind that I had only jerry-rigged an experimental solution for the first season game and had no real experience. Nonetheless, my entrepreneurial instincts prevailed. I bet on myself. I had made it this far, so I would deliver with ingenuity and hard work. While the suits were pleased, the racetrack's horses gave me the final approval as they extended their necks from their stalls to bite at the thick fog keeping them cool.

When I finally retired from football, I poured all my focus into Cloudburst to determine if it could go the distance. After developing some marketing material and uncovering a few sales, I knew I couldn't fly solo. Enter neighbor Mike Davis, who matched my sales abilities with his brain for numbers. My very own Dustin Hoffman in *Rain Man*. We worked like a well-oiled machine with Mike hanging close to the business while I was out selling . . . a natural gift from Dad. But we both put on our inventor hats, too, and spent countless hours in the garage creating and fine-tuning different misting pieces until we could secure factory space and a full team.

I also assembled a board of advisors to offer insights from their professional successes and failures. Their real-world experiences far exceeded any off-the-shelf business book, and I heeded much of their guidance. There were few formal entry requirements for my little club. They just had to be someone I admired and respected for their business acumen and perseverance, many not in a related industry. Unlike a board of directors, these wise sages never sought compensation but instead freely dispensed their wisdom over long coffee sessions or extended dinners. I discovered they sought the positive reinforcement of watching the next entrepreneur absorb and act on their advice.

One of my advisors became a great friend with our respective businesses flourishing in harmony. He owned a retail sales company that connected Cloudburst and other small businesses with big box stores. His team would keep the shelves full and orders coming our way. He was a dream advisor, friend, and partner wrapped in one.

Our big break came when we pitched to the 1996 Summer Olympic Committee in Atlanta. As small as we were, we went for it, believing we could cool the largest sporting event in the history of the world, yet we hadn't even handled a town fair. That was blind confidence, and it paid off. We were David competing against

Goliath, a.k.a. General Electric, and many others, so we did our thing, thanked the committee, and flew back to California. As far as we were concerned, the mere fact that we went for it was worthy of celebration. Two weeks later, much to our shock, we were awarded the contract for the Summer Olympics, which would turn out to be the hottest Olympic games on record.

How the heck did we land this gig? During the pitch in Atlanta, I noticed a face on the committee that looked vaguely familiar. But I was so focused on hitting every pitch point that I avoided any distractions. As it turns out, one of the key decision-makers was Mike Arellano, the director of field operations. He met me years prior in the Raiders' locker room when he was a football cleat salesman for an emerging brand. Few paid attention, and he was dismissed outright by most; however, I noticed his effort and wanted to make sure he didn't leave the locker room discouraged. I offered to try the cleats, and I distinctly recall his gratitude. This was karma: doing the right thing to help someone else without thinking about how I could benefit. Because I showed support for Mike Arellano all those years ago, he was now offering it in return. We just needed to deliver. And we did it through sheer will and nonstop work.

It was a monumental undertaking involving seventeen days of Olympic games. Plus, there were the opening and closing ceremonies and a week on the front and back end with far more venues involved than we anticipated, including Miami, Orlando, Birmingham, Athens, and Washington DC. We needed to grow our team fast, so we grabbed a few available hands, including my brother and Mike's dad. But, in all honesty, we needed far more, given the magnitude of the task in front of us.

I knew we were in the trenches of servicing the Olympics when we were directed into the bowels of a 1.5 million square foot underground garage to a roped-off quadrant. I'm pretty sure it hadn't experienced fresh air since its build. We spent the next five days in this humid hellhole unpacking and assembling our equipment and positioning it around the cities and stadiums. Each night, we would meet to share our notes and play one round of Rochambeau to determine who would trek overnight to service some issue at one of the venues. Meanwhile, the rest of us grabbed about four hours of sleep to maintain our sanity throughout the games.

Decathlete Gold Medalist Dan O'Brien Cooling with Cloudburst

We would forget all the challenging work and exhaustion when one of these elite athletes would use our equipment between matches or events. To see them in all their magnificence and strength was breathtaking. One night, while we were decompressing and reveling in our progress during the games, we were jolted to attention by breaking news that startled everyone in the bar, at the games, and around the world. A pipe bomb detonated in the Centennial Olympic Park, and within an instant, the games and their memory were stained forevermore. I recall fighting back tears in the crowded bar, but eventually, they flooded my eyes just like so many other people that night.

Cloudburst Team at the Olympics

We also developed a retail product line called Mist & Cool that landed Home Depot with the support of West Coast President Harry Pierce. He opened the door and gave us some much-needed coaching, but he was crisp with his subsequent message: "Don't fuck this up." I spent ridiculous amounts of time in Home Depot stores across the West Coast training employees, running demonstrations, and chatting with potential customers. The news got back to Harry that Cloudburst hustled and put in the effort across the region, but the best performance indicator was our sales numbers.

After the success of the Olympics and Home Depot picking up steam along with Costco, Target, Lowes, and others, we decided it was time to refresh our business plan. With a crisp rewrite in hand, I took to the skies to check on a few new opportunities. On my return trip home from Texas, just as we were taxiing to the runway, monsoon-style rain began to fall in sheets, and we were grounded on the tarmac for three hours. At the start of this waiting period, I felt my claustrophobia stirring, and I began counting the minutes, hoping we would deplane soon.

Sensing my discomfort, the gentleman seated next to me piped up. "I hope you aren't in a hurry today," he said as he flashed me a kind smile and pushed his small wire frames back from the end of his nose.

We fell into conversation, introducing ourselves and discussing our business ventures. Walter Lim, I learned, was the founder and CEO of a sizeable aerosol company in Los Angeles. I explained Cloudburst, and he was interested in learning more as he leaned in. It was time for us to order cocktails.

"What markets are you looking to expand?" he asked as he sipped his vodka tonic.

I pulled out our business plan, and the dialog took on a life of its own, lasting the length of our travel time. By the end of our flight, it was clear that Cloudburst could be a good investment opportunity for Walter, given the adjacency of our businesses. In the following weeks, we stayed connected, and ultimately, he became our biggest investor. My good fortune was at work again, especially since less than 1 percent of new companies secure venture capital. I'm pretty sure that our business plan went everywhere with me from that point forward. It was a classic reminder of what's possible when preparation meets opportunity.

Along with a healthy dose of good fortune, other doors opened to protect me. In one case, the door revealed itself under the guise of randomness, but, in fact, the universe put it in my path for a very good reason. On a whim, or so I thought, I enrolled in a stock trading course through INVESTools called "Thinkorswim." Why not? I was interested and figured it would be a great chance to get an education on the stock market. I came from a financially conservative family who leaned more on a real estate and savings account model, so I had zero foundation in stocks.

I ate it up and found myself diving deeper into *CNBC*, *The Wall Street Journal*, and other business news feeds each morning, followed by a heavy dose of course homework each week. If my neighbors heard through the walls, they would've been convinced that I was stalking *CNBC*'s Jim Cramer as I listened to him the way that an evangelist listens to the radio. I would shout back at the screen and go coffee-to-coffee with him all day, riding on a caffeine high that propelled me late into the evenings. Fortunately, the jitters would finally wear off just in time for bed each night as I examined the futures for an early sign of the next day's trajectory. That's right; I was hooked on the market.

As I increased my understanding and thought more about day trading, I started to notice concerning trends in early 2007, or maybe it was the start of adrenal failure, given the consumption of far too much coffee over the last six months. Whatever it was, it manifested as a strange sensation in my gut, suggesting that things were close to caving in. When I could no longer ignore it, I contacted my portfolio manager and told him to sell everything that I had in the market by the end of the week and transfer it all to my savings account, where it sat idle but protected for the next year and a half.

"Everything?" my advisor questioned.

"Yes, everything, Joe, and have it all into my savings account by the end of the week," I rattled off with coffee jitters in full force. Meanwhile, Jim Cramer barked on my computer screen in the background as I wondered if a week was truly realistic.

"But Steve, that's a radical move right now. I wouldn't advise it," he stated as I worked to adjust the volume of *CNBC* and looked for my notes on the prior week's performance. My coffee mug tipped over onto my papers as I found what I was looking for. I took it as another sign that I was to trust my gut.

"Thanks for your advice, Joe, but I've thought long and hard about this one," I said tersely with the certainty of a surgeon. Joe didn't know I had taken this investing course, and I figured I shouldn't muddy the waters by informing him that I had gone rogue. I could already tell he was trying to walk me back from the ledge with his "let the professionals handle this one" shtick.

"Steve, seriously, where's this coming from?" Joe was attempting his best therapist play as I heard him settle into his leather chair.

"Joe, my life has been about keeping things positive and hoping for the best, but I also trust my gut, and this isn't going to end well," I explained. "I need to protect my nest egg, and the best way, right now, is to get off this disintegrating perch." I had no idea where this analogy originated, but it worked.

"All right, Steve. I'm going to need a little more time than a week. Remember this conversation the next time we connect, okay?" he said with a touch of condescension.

"You got it, Joe. I most certainly will," I said, knowing I would never talk to Joe again the way I spoke to Cramer every day.

This cheap course, along with my gut and the universe, aligned at just the right time to save my funds. I was one of the lucky ones yet again. By 2009, things were looking up when I came across a list of the fifty best wealth managers in the country. Scanning the magazine, I found one close by in Orange County. In my first meeting with Laila Pence, I knew I was in the hands of an exceptional advisor who cared for each client. Along with protecting my financial future, Laila became a dear friend and has been in my corner while her star continues to rise.

CHAPTER 8:

THE SEEKER

If I were to pick any small town in America that matched my health and wellness-centric values, it would be Malibu. It isn't uncommon for my tribe to discuss innovative exercises, the latest biohacks, or new treatments to optimize our health. While it sometimes goes a bit extreme, the intent that drives these conversations resonates. I don't profess to be an expert, but I stayed healthy throughout my life and explored many different practices. Experimenting and listening to my body has worked well for me.

When I talk about health, I often make a comparison to a car since many people are diligent about caring for their ride. I monitor the fuel going into the tank, warm it up gradually, tend to the parts in need, and periodically flush the lines to keep it clean because I'm proud of it. I want to feel good when I take it out.

My fueling philosophy has adjusted many times throughout my life, but it's always aligned with my goals. As a young guy, all I wanted was to increase in size, so I blindly shoveled food without attention to nutritional value. I discovered nothing was out of bounds if it could help me gain weight. My college teammate, whose family managed a large herd of cattle, shared a special high-protein recipe they fed newborn calves to help them develop. All I heard was high protein and I was onboard, so he dropped off a heavy burlap sack with a rope tie and a cow diagram on the side. This was a little different than the protein powders I came across in the health-food stores of Minneapolis.

Yet, undeterred, I found the one line of directions that were rather straightforward: pour contents into a large metal bucket and stir with a wire whisk. This was straight-off-the-farm shit. Then I found a tagline stating that the low lactose content reduced the incidence of diarrhea in cows. How far would I go to put on muscle? This was a test, and I was starting to question my sanity. In the end, I pressed on, holding back my gag reflex, while I managed to put on a few pounds.

This fueling philosophy extended into my Cowboys years when I saddled up to all-you-can-eat sirloin steak dinners and devoured herds of cattle. It would be logical to expect NFL teams to encourage and offer healthy meals, but the Raiders proved to be unique again, at the buffet table this time. During my first pregame breakfast with my new team, I was shocked to see five-gallon vats of ice cream with all the toppings at the end of the line. Assorted flavors, chocolate sauces, and whipped cream all to be consumed five hours before taking the field. When I questioned the trainers about the fifteen gallons of ice cream, they shrugged. "Al wants it the way it's always been done. It's tradition." I later saw a couple of teammates with rabid-dog cottonmouth sniffing on ammonia caps in the third quarter to stay sharp. I knew they weren't out of shape but rather enjoyed too much of their fudge sundae.

When I hit my mid-career stride with the Raiders, my attention turned to longevity. Since my career depended on my body's health, I got more serious about this complex machine. I started using a nutritionist to methodically plan and portion more nutrient-dense meals. This included employing Dr. Philip Goglia's training and nutrition background to organize three meals and three snacks a day to maintain a solid 300 pounds. Fast-forward to my post-career life, I no longer needed or wanted to maintain my bulk, so I adopted a plant-based diet and leaned out. Without getting into labels and restrictions, it would be fair to say that I'm just shy of a card-carrying vegan at this point in my life. My younger self, slurping my baby cow formula, wouldn't believe it.

I never considered any of my eating programs a diet. I have a visceral reaction to the word because food is meant to be enjoyed, and we sometimes forget that part. I doubt many athletes say they need to diet and work out. They eat and train. As one looks around, diet programs abound, but humanity continues to balloon. Obesity was an outlier up into the 1970s, and then deceptive labeling, poor-quality foods, and corn syrup opened addictive doors that society has been unable to close.

I've always loved these two sayings: "You can't outrun your fork," and "Nothing tastes as good as fit feels." Eighty-five percent of weight management is through my mouth, not training. No matter how hard I exercise for at least an hour a day, I still need to manage the other twenty-three hours, not filling it with sugars and other dead carbohydrates. I know my eating plan and do my best to stick with it, but if I veer off and junk out, I make the necessary course adjustment and don't wait until Monday to regroup. I jump back on the plan the following day.

More recently, I embraced time-restricted eating, which has kept me disciplined. This approach allows me to eat as much as I want during my eating window so I don't feel deprived. Plus, it's a repeatable pattern that offers my body the predictability it craves. Every day, I enjoy my first meal around 7 a.m. and my last bite, usually protein, no later than 2 p.m. This gives my body more than enough time to digest everything and burn through my glucose, which lasts roughly twelve hours. Now my body is creating ketones to use my fat as fuel and feed my mitochondria. It was a bit of a struggle initially, but the desire to munch on something fades once I drink plenty of water to squelch the hunger. Since the eating window is so short, I focus on consuming high-octane fuel, not empty carbohydrates, which leave me begging for more.

How do I have a social life with this kind of eating plan? Well, it takes compassionate friends who are understanding and enjoy our time together more than the food part of the equation. That said, sometimes I pause the pattern for nights of entertainment or vacations. In the end, it's worthwhile to resume my program after all the fun.

The topic of fuel would be incomplete without addressing supplements. My views have evolved as I no longer take any supplements beyond Doctor's Best Glucosamine Chondroitin & MSM with Opti MSM, Mountain Rose ground organic turmeric, testosterone, and protein shakes. The third on the list is a loaded topic, so let me start with the one-two punch of joint lubrication and natural anti-inflammatory properties that support my active lifestyle. With beach running, paddle surfing, and everything else, I know my joints feel better when they get the added treatment of Doctor's Best and Mountain Rose. This is a far cry from all the supplements I took in my playing days. I downed fistfuls of capsules multiple times daily upon the recommendation of well-intended colleagues and friends. These weren't illicit drugs, just their suggestions.

Now for the stigmatized good stuff, testosterone. Over the last ten years, I benefited from using prescription testosterone cream with semiannual blood tests to check my prostate-specific antigen and testosterone levels. I like to hover on the higher end of the testosterone range for my age group. As a result, I recover faster, have more energy, and feel confident whatever the hour. What's not to love? I think this hormone supplementation gets a bad rap because of those who abuse it. Like all good things, too much is never a wise idea. But, with measured use, I offer my body this much-needed hormone proven to wane as we age.

Protein shakes are another story. I love them so much that I would request one as my last meal on death row. I've tried countless brands and eventually migrated from whey to plant protein sources. My meal replacement shake goes down the hatch each morning. Most days, I also have one additional shake two hours after my last meal to keep me satiated and achieve my daily goal of consuming at least 200 grams of protein. These shakes ensure I get the highest quality, most nutritionally dense meal to complement my food consumption.

Cue the most asked question of vegans: is plant protein as good as animal protein? Take a look at a gorilla or buffalo; they subsist on plants and still appear quite beastly.

Each morning, I wake within five minutes of 4:30 a.m., including the weekends. It isn't so much by choice, but my circadian rhythm is so consistent that my body is ready to start the day that early. Even as a kid, I rose with the sun, but for the last twenty years, 4:30 a.m. seems to be the sweet spot. I love the early stillness that grounds me and helps set my intentions for the day. Before I begin my meditation, I drink twenty ounces of warm water with a tablespoon of baking soda and apple cider vinegar. Besides how it strongly encourages my morning movement—we'll get to that topic later—it alkalizes my body as I kick-start my day.

After thirty minutes of meditation, I move on to warming up my brain with the app *Elevate*, which fires up my mind and exercises it like a muscle. I've tried all sorts of applications and programs, but *Elevate* is the only one that I've found helpful. Once the inside work is done, I turn to some outdoor cardio to get my body moving with twenty minutes of high-intensity work. In the last five years, I focused on training in pools to get my heart rate cranked in the early morning, but beach and stair runs worked just as well over the years. The book *Body for Life* by Bill Phillips encourages completing morning cardio in a fasted state to get into the fat stores. It's proven to shed fat 40 percent faster if performed as directed. It's always worked for me and is hands down my easiest path to shed a few pounds fast.

In 2016, I was looking for ways to up my fitness regimen and get out of my comfort zone when I discovered Extreme Performance Training (XPT) and joined Malibu locals Laird Hamilton and Gabby Reece for their three-day immersion in Mexico. I was exposed to intense water-based weight training, next-level breath work, and the classic contrasting heat and ice protocols as part of recovery. The setting was fantastic, but the people made it special. I was surrounded by like-minded individuals who thrived on pushing themselves and testing their perceived limitations. It helped that Laird, a big wave surfer, and Gabby, a former professional volleyball player, were top athletes and celebrities in their respective fields, but that was just the icing on the cake. The bond formed with these two was immediate, and after the event concluded, they invited me to train with their local tribe back in Malibu.

For the next several years, I spent six days a week training with a remarkable tribe at Laird and Gabby's compound, a sort of fitness Camelot. Once I entered the gate to their home in the hills of Malibu, overlooking the vast Pacific Ocean, I descended to the outdoor training facility. It included one of the largest and deepest private pools in Southern California along with ice tubs, oversized saunas, and a bevy of fitness equipment to round out each day's session. Everything about it was extraordinary, and that was just the stuff.

The people who were members of the tribe elevated the space with their magnetic energy. It was an eclectic group of successful guys who were all leaders in their respective fields but always entered the compound on equal footing. These were Olympic and professional athletes, film producers, actors, artists, business leaders, and more. Everyone dropped their ego at the gate and supported each other as we pushed the envelope.

The "extreme" in XPT carried over to their home pool, as I quickly discovered. Not too many of us made it out without a story or two. Though we tried to keep a close eye on one another, accidents happened. I recall one morning when I was working underwater with a partner running with 50-pound weights twelve feet below the surface. My partner was short on air, and as he shot for the surface to get some much-needed oxygen, he passed out two feet shy of his target. I was just yards from him as I saw his extremities go limp. The weights dropped like depth finders, and within a second, a burly arm plunged through the water and grabbed a fistful of hair to yank him from the pool. I hit the surface to see Laird resuscitating him along the pool's edge. The quick grab was critical, as it prevented him from swallowing water that would've choked him as he regained consciousness. Much to my surprise, the waterman was back in the pool a few repetitions later as if nothing had transpired.

Then there were days one assumed would be easy but dialed up unexpectedly. One morning, I was performing a simple series with Laird that included hot and cold contrasts to generate shock proteins. It involved a harmless two minutes in the sauna, followed by another two minutes in the ice bath, rinse, and repeat. No sweat, or so I thought. Then Laird cranked up the sauna to 220 degrees Fahrenheit and pulled an assault bike into the space. I was to ride as hard as possible in the scorching heat with a ski hat on to keep my head from burning and a pair of oven mitts to protect my hands from the scalding grips of the bike. It was also wise to shut my eyes so as not to singe my lids from the heat kicked up by the bike. It was quite a sight, but the intent was to test the body with extreme heat and cardio intensity, and this fit the bill.

Once the two minutes in the brutal heat concluded, I burst out the doors and jumped into a tub that had a foot-thick layer of ice. I've seen plenty of folks attempt to mimic this with a tray of ice cubes in their cold bathtub, but that's nowhere near the freeze that comes from sinking into an excessive amount of cubes for two minutes. Every bit of the body goes completely numb. As I reached the point of freezing that involved an odd burning sensation,

Ice Bath

I knew I was just over the two-minute mark. After repeating this cycle eight times, I stumbled off the bike, trying to avoid searing my leg on the metal shaft. I was delirious from the heat that felt like an inescapable oven. In my haze, I landed on the bike handle, which immediately reminded me of what wins when metal and bone collide.

I spent the next several weeks nursing a broken rib, and honestly, I was relieved to take a break from this sequence. Being certifiably maimed was the only reasonable excuse to miss time with this tribe.

We also performed many breathing exercises that were quite intense over extended periods. Think pranayama yoga on steroids. Many of us lost consciousness at one time or another, especially after sessions that lasted over an hour. Losing consciousness was a rite of passage, but one time, for me, it went even further. I was lying on the gym floor as Laird ran us through a rapid series of more aggressive breaths. We protruded our bellies on the in-breath followed by a fast and hard exhale, ensuring a full release of carbon dioxide. I was always one to put in my best effort and was blowing out my air with all the force I could muster.

After twenty minutes, I looked up at the ceiling and silently debated how many more sets Laird had in him. This guy could go, and I mean really push it, longer than any human I ever encountered. I closed my eyes and submitted to the process, ratcheting up my force even further. If he was going to press it to the max, I would follow his lead. Just as the thought receded, I felt a strange popping sensation in my stomach, right under my belly button. It was an unusual sensation, but I assumed this was one of the byproducts of aggressive training for an extended timeframe.

The feeling brought me back to the moment I popped my ACL during a game against Buffalo. Since I lived without that ACL repair, I assumed that whatever went down in my abdomen was at worse a hernia and at best a strained muscle. Later that day, I started to notice some swelling in my belly and began to fear the worst. I had breathed my way to a fricking hernia. Now how was I going to explain that to my wife and doctor? As I rehearsed it in my mind, it still sounded insane. One semi-successful surgery later, I was on my way toward an extended recovery.

The warning signs of bodily harm were there all along, including another morning when a buddy emerged from the deep end of the pool looking for the tip of his finger. Like everyone else before him, he was numb to the pain, at least initially. The thirty-five-pound weight had dropped on his digit and severed the end off, but that didn't stop him from resuming pool training less than two weeks later, just an ounce or two lighter.

Along with the sick enjoyment of pushing ourselves, many times a bit too far, a brotherhood formed that went beyond any depth I experienced in professional football. Every topic we discussed in the truth barrel, a.k.a. the sauna, was at a profoundly analytical level, with everyone thoughtfully contributing to the topic of the day: from poetry to mitochondrial function, nothing was off limits except for politics. These dudes were thinkers and smart beyond their prescribed domains. We shared books, philosophies, and more health tips than I can count. My body was worked, and my mind was fed. It was a memorable time in my life, but once the pandemic struck in 2020, much of the tribe dissolved. As with everything else in my life, I honor the memories and bonds formed in this Camelot of fitness.

Meeting of the Minds in the Sauna

When not working out with my tribe, I often rely on a basic lifting program that includes the pyramid approach of higher repetition using less weight moving to lower reps with heavier weight. No matter what exercise or body part I focus on, this is a decent roadmap. When following this approach, I lift weights six days a week, heavier for three of those days and lighter for the remainder.

Only a few post-career injuries threw me off my weightlifting protocol. One of which was a torn shoulder and bicep repair in 2020. I was lucky enough to get the Los Angeles Lakers team surgeon who specializes in shoulders. I was warned about a six-month recovery, but I treated it like my job to rebound quickly. It started with heat, not ice, post-surgery. This went against conventional wisdom and what I was taught from peewee league all the way through the NFL, but new research suggested that applying heat instead of ice can be more helpful for recovery. It worked well for me. I would encourage anyone facing joint surgery to investigate the studies against using ice. Long story short, I was back paddle surfing, weightlifting, and everything else in three months.

How does a guy from Minnesota end up paddle surfing? One of the greatest passions of my life didn't arrive on the scene until well into my fifties. Surfing, as I discovered, was the perfect union of my values, life philosophy, and lifestyle. Sure, I spent decades living in Southern California beach towns where I admired the surf culture from a distance, but I never saw myself as one of them. Maybe it was my size or fear of sharks, but whatever stopped me, it was shortsighted. Thankfully, a fortuitous move brought surfing to my front yard.

When Lizzy and I joined forces, we landed a beachfront apartment at the bottom of a main drag in Manhattan Beach. It was an eyesore of a building, but the location couldn't be better. Each morning, I watched a dozen surfers about my age meet outside our window with their coffee and surfboards, rain or shine. From what I could observe, they appeared to be a tight gang I would love to join, so I thought of a way to approach them with the utmost respect and class. I picked up a couple dozen donuts, and I was in; it worked like a charm. I was now a member of the Marine Street Crabs.

Most of these guys had been standing at that corner every morning for over thirty years. They told stories about their antics back in elementary school together. It was the West Coast version of the buddies from my childhood. The only significant divergence was the prominence of surf instead of hockey. In addition to reminiscing and swapping stories, the Crabs would keep an eye on the surf conditions as they downed their coffee. Sprinkled among the stories were pauses to point to a wave or comment about a good surfer in the lineup. Finally, they would check out the girls running by before deciding whether to suit up and surf or head home to the wife and kids before work. More often than not, surf prevailed.

The Crabs were patient with me as I learned the ropes that summer. I purchased my first board and jumped in feetfirst to join my new gang as I took to paddle surfing. The initial sessions were a bit challenging, with a dozen well-intended coaches, but it was my first egress from the water that I'll never forget. My overconfidence may have been to blame when I paddled back to shore, expecting a smooth exit. Yet, as I prepared to dismount, the tiniest reverberation from the shore hit my board and sent me tumbling. I fell awkwardly into a short foot of water and blew my elbow bursa sac. I was one hour into a new sport and already needed to see a doctor.

Things only improved from there. . . . How could they not? But there was still one nagging issue that I was challenged to address, and I blame my fascination with the movie *Jaws*. Every time I was out on the water, I was distracted, scanning the surface for dark shadows. I told myself that it was a mind-over-matter fix, but trying to ignore it only brought it to the forefront. And I couldn't talk to the other surfers about sharks because it was taboo. We didn't need to conceive, believe, and achieve their presence in our shore break.

Like most things, education was ultimately the answer. All the research suggested that the six-foot juvenile great white sharks in our bay weren't interested in humans. In fact, they came to shallow waters for safety and to consume stingrays, which was a nagging problem around the beach. In the end, a stingray, not a shark, did the most damage. Lizzy, who's tough as nails, was withering in pain when the venom of a stingray barb pierced through her foot. Multiple doctor visits and a surgery later, she recovered but now welcomes the sharks because they rid our shores of those nasty stingrays.

Eventually, I lost my fear of these apex predators after paddling over six-footers regularly. I only had one run-in that left me shaken. Lizzy and I were paddling single file a quarter mile from shore when I saw a sizable shadow beneath me and assumed that a large cloud overhead was causing the darkness. I looked up and suddenly tensed because there wasn't a single cloud in sight. As I continued to paddle, I peered behind me just as a large dorsal fin penetrated the surface. A shark was evaluating us, and it was no juvenile. I was close enough to see considerable scars from deep gashes and a few spots where the smooth line of the fin looked ragged with sections missing. This shark was battle-worn, not confused.

"Paddle straight in, baby," I said, trying to keep my cool.

"I don't want to go in yet," she snapped, but then she turned around and saw the expression of dread on my face.

"A shark is tracking us. Paddle hard," I said.

The fight or flight switch was hit, and Lizzy accelerated her paddle strokes, beelining it for shore but also angling to be in the line of sight of the nearest lifeguard stand to document our potential demise. No matter what I did, my legs wouldn't stop shaking until I hit the sand.

I hightailed it to the guard, and within ten minutes, a Coast Guard helicopter was deployed to track the shark overhead while a boat worked in tandem. The ship launched a water cannon across the surface to push the shark out of the shallows and back to the nearly 3,000-foot canyon beyond the bay where it belonged. It was quite a scene and a good reminder that we're in their backyard.

Once I shook the incident from my mind, I was back in the water.

I took comfort in the fact that not a single surfer had been attacked in Manhattan Beach in recent memory, just an accidental bite of a swimmer off the pier in 2014. While surfing isn't without risks, the same could be said for driving on the freeways around Los Angeles. I can honestly say that no matter what happens on the water, I'm always glad I went, even that day.

Winter Surf in Manhattan Beach, CA

Not long after I took up paddle surfing, I joined my buddy, Laird, at his place in Kauai. It was like going from T-ball to batting practice with Babe Ruth. I couldn't believe my good fortune to learn from the best. As it turns out, it would be more accurate to say that I watched the best do his thing while I tried to keep up. That said, I learned fast, grew a lot, and had a blast.

Board Meeting with Laird

I knew going in that Laird operates at one speed, and I was going to be going 90 mph all weekend just trying to keep up. Every morning, we woke at 4:30 a.m., tossed back straight coconut oil, and dropped butter into our coffee as we headed out the door. Fats were the high-octane fuel of choice. It was a far cry from my coffee, vegan protein shake, and morning meditation, but this man functioned on fats and adrenaline, which seemed to work for him, so why not test out his morning routine? I wasn't there to question his methods and was too focused on keeping pace, so I would be in the passenger seat of his black monster truck when he bolted out of the driveway.

Since it was still pitch-dark when we grabbed the boards, I wrongfully assumed that there were a few stops in store before catching waves at dawn. At 4:50 a.m., Laird cranked the truck off the road and deep into the trees, stopping by the water's edge. Before I could react, he grabbed his board, secured his leg strap, and launched into the abyss. Meanwhile, the coffee was finally hitting, and my mind was awash with questions and concerns. *How will I know where to go in the dark? Sharks feed in the early morning, right? Is it too late to fake an injury? And last, but most important: what the fuck have I gotten myself into?*

I shook my head and searched within to summon whatever shards of confidence I could patch together. I bit hard on my inner cheek and grabbed my board as I entered the dark waters that accompany every ocean-based horror flick I know. I had to stay on my board to avoid the appearance of large bait for the predators below the surface. Plus, I needed to make up some serious time to reach Laird and avoid drifting too far into open water.

With the waves pounding the boulders, I fell off my board five feet from shore and couldn't touch the bottom. Wherever I was, it was over a shelf, and guess what feeds near the drop-offs? This was precisely the situation that I wanted to avoid. I shook my head and started the positive self-talk, but honestly, it took all I could muster to stay focused. After about the tenth fall into the dark water, I finally heard Laird's chatter in the distance. Between my steady heart rate of 180 beats per minute and the waves tossing me around, I was beyond exhausted when Laird came into view.

Over the course of our time on the water, several of his buddies joined to surf and left after a few hours. And then another round came and went, so I knew we were nearly four hours into our session when Laird finally slowed down to a normal human's pace. I motioned that I was heading for the truck, where I recovered for the next two hours until he finally shot into shore. For the next couple of days, that was the routine. It was a sink-or-swim education, but I still loved it and will always appreciate the opportunity to grow.

The situation in Kauai wasn't the last time I got in over my head. In most cases, it comes down to miscalculation, which I work hard to avoid. However, when it's guys like Laird or, better yet, my wife, I defy my good judgment. We were living in Huntington Beach, known for its great surf, and Lizzy was eager to get in the water after a week in the office. When we hit the beach, we were greeted by fast-approaching fog that enveloped the entire area. I could barely make out the lifeguard tower, let alone hear whatever they were projecting over the loudspeaker.

Once down by the water's edge, we stretched out and strapped the boards to our ankles as I pointed to a stake in the ground with a sign reading, *High Surf Warning, Surfing Not Advised*. Lizzy shrugged and lifted her board. That's one thing about my wife that I've learned to love: when she's on a mission, very little will deter her.

With visibility no more than fifty feet and my commonsense meter redlining, we entered the water. As we waded out, I was hit with a strong current that challenged my balance. The waves felt thicker than usual and were carrying more power. Meanwhile, Lizzy plowed ahead as she spied an opening between waves, but it was hard to tell in all the dense fog. Within two minutes, I had no idea where to find Lizzy as I scrambled to retrieve my board. Just when I found it, another set rolled through, and I was back to square one.

I finally made it out, but I still couldn't see or hear Lizzy in the pounding surf. Focusing on locating her was now a top priority, but not paying attention to heavy surf was a great way to get in trouble. Trouble for me came in a set of five heavy waves. After enduring just enough beatdowns to nearly break my soul, it was over, and the water calmed. I reeled my board in to find only half attached to my leash. The board had broken in two. So now I was unsure of my distance from shore as I floated on half a board with Lizzy nowhere to be found. I knew this was a bad idea.

A few minutes later, I heard a whistle and saw Lizzy emerging from the mist, completely unscathed and smiling. "Where have you been? I've been waiting," she stated with some undue emphasis on the waiting part.

"Well, Mrs. Short on Common Sense, I lost you along with half my board back there," I said, happy that we were both okay.

"Guilty," Lizzy said sheepishly, aware that her smarts didn't always extend beyond the books. "Next time, you make the call." It was a good lesson, and we left wiser for it. The call that I made next was to a surf camp.

With all the variables in surfing, I knew some excellent coaching would save me a lot of pain that trial and error dished out during my first few experiences on the water. I ended up at a surf camp in Fiji on the island of Namotu, taught by Hawaiian waterman Dave Kalama who invented modern paddle surfing with Laird. "Kalama Kamps," as they're called, gave me a good education. I was so excited about this trip that as the camp start date drew near, I indulged in a custom-made paddle surfboard. I was basically bringing a Ferrari, and I figured this could only help me excel.

With Waterman Dave Kalama

Namotu was an idyllic setting: a tiny island surrounded by nearly half a dozen pristine surf breaks with nothing but waves and fresh seafood for as long as I could stay awake. I was in heaven the minute I set foot on the island. Since it was the first morning of camp, a couple of us who were new to Namotu were asked to paddle out with one of the coaches for a basic water briefing. As we followed like little ducklings paddling out into the vast blue ocean, our instructor guided us beyond the surf break about a quarter mile offshore. He was positioned looking out to the open ocean, and we had all eyes glued on him. Just as he launched into his advice, his eyes widened in sync with an alarming command to get up fast because a sweeper was coming.

"What's a sweeper?" I yelled over the rumble of the incoming surf, but it was too late for questions.

Lesson one was in full swing. I learned quickly about sweeper waves that morning. These rare occurrences extend past the reef with a much wider swath. They generally take everyone by surprise unless you're paying close attention. Given the tone of the instructor's command, I knew it wasn't a drill, so I went into survival mode, having no clue how to handle the situation. *If I dive too deep, will I hit the reef? But will I go over the falls if I don't dive deep enough?* There was no one to ask and no time to debate. This ten-foot sweeper blew everyone into oblivion . . . what surfers call a yard sale. Bodies and boards were flying everywhere as leashes snapped and appendages flailed in the mountain of whitewash. It was pure chaos.

All I cared about was Lizzy. I spotted her about twenty-five yards away as I came up for air. To say she was bug-eyed would be an understatement. She was in one piece but had no board, paddle, or leash and was waving her arms to get my attention as the whitewash engulfed her like a snowdrift. I grabbed my leash to reel in my board, only to discover half of it was missing and riding out its life in the white foam. So much for my Ferrari . . . another board bites the dust.

Once I got over to Lizzy, I could see that she was shell-shocked and giggling uncomfortably as she does when she's nervous. "What have we gotten ourselves into?" she wondered aloud.

Welcome to Namotu; school was now in session.

After Kalama Kamp, I was hooked on paddle surfing and wanted to spend more time in the water. Never one to hold back on speaking or acting on a feeling, I admired this one surfer's ability out in front of our Manhattan Beach pad and met him as he exited the water. I had been watching this new face around the beach and thought, *Why not pick his brain?* I'm so thankful that I almost always listen to my gut instinct and act, mostly because I don't want to live with regrets. So, out of the thousands of paddle surfers I could approach along our coastline, I had no idea I was about to chat up the world champion, Sean Poynter.

Sean greeted me with a smile and talked like he had all the time in the world to share his insights on the sport. He also mentioned that he ran a surf camp in Mexico along with the Australian Ian "Kanga" Cairns, a premier power surfer. Enough said, I was in on the next camp. While I always believed in the adage that you're the sum of the five people you hang out with, I could only wish to be the sum of these two studs when it comes to surfing. This was a fun but more serious camp than Namotu.

Ian didn't mess around. He was old school and full of expletives when he barked instructions while riding his board like a raging bull in the wave behind me. He reminded me of Mike Ditka during my football days. He had a good heart but a tough exterior, and he dished out unfiltered feedback in short barks. Meanwhile, Sean was a precise and clean technician. He surfed as an artist carving beautiful lines and offering insights with thought and careful consideration. They were like the two guys from *The Odd Couple*, but they were a great blend of skills and styles. With the camps in Fiji and Mexico under my belt, I was in a much better position to navigate this new sport.

In my early years of surfing, I didn't realize just how lucky I was to avoid serious injury while out in the surf. Mother Blue, as I like to call the ocean, forces respect if it isn't offered. I've watched leashes wrap around all sorts of body parts, including necks and fingers, and fins slice bodies with the ease of a Ginsu knife. I watched one guy pop up from a wipeout cradling his bloody hand minus two fingertips. Meanwhile, my neighbor slashed his neck on his board's fins, and

Lizzy broke her forearm at the close-out of a major swell, referred to as Code Red 2. Yes, a swell big enough to have its own name. More on that later.

The most ironic part is that Mother Blue is also well-known for her healing effects, so like all things, she giveth and taketh. She lights me up with uncontrollable energy or lets me know that it isn't my day. Not too many hobbies fire up my brain as much as surfing. My head is hard at work, given the constantly changing water surface and the relational positioning of other surfers. Then add on the need to focus on balance, foot positioning, and, of course, wave timing... all that for just one wave. It's a combined mind and body effort.

When a major swell from the southern hemisphere makes its way toward the California shores, it's game on. These are generally winter storms (the northern hemisphere's summer) that I track off the east coast of New Zealand in the violent Tasmin Sea that travel 7,000 unimpeded miles and light up our coastline. The surfers in my area glue themselves to forecasting applications like *Surfline*, which heighten the excitement. Once the timing of the swell's arrival is imminent, I clear my calendar of appointments since Mother Blue is on her time, and when she offers waves, you surf. As for physical preparation, I lay off the weights about a week out and focus on yoga and stretching versus heavy lifting and cardio. I also spend a lot of time using my Theragun, which is an amazing preparation and recovery tool developed by my good buddy, Dr. Jason Wersland. There's nothing worse than being too tight or sore to get back out on the water.

The last monster swell of 2022 surprised everyone with her veracity and was labeled a Code Red by the Tahitian government as it passed through, heading for Southern California. Code Red means that all boats and watercraft are banned from traveling in the surrounding area. By the time this swell hit California, it was much bigger than predicted by the professionals and unofficially named Code Red Two. Since I live on a great surf point, all my buddies started texting for live reports as she drew near. The start of this chatter is like kids preparing for Christmas. The good juju flows, and spirits are high.

Over the course of a swell that typically lasts three to five days, memories are made, bonds grow tighter, and abilities improve, but plenty of pain is delivered as well. Equipment snaps and blood spills from collisions with the boards or rocky bottoms. By the end, everyone is drained. Once the swell moves on, it's literally the quiet after the storm. We all need a break to reminisce, swap stories, and lick our wounds.

Paddle Surfing

Part of my recovery process includes eliminating distractions so my body can focus on repair. It may sound wacky, but I discovered that keeping my digestive tract in great shape helps redirect attention where it's needed most. This offbeat obsession drove me to invent an unconventional toilet that I hold a patent for, The Courtesy 180. The idea came to me while traveling through Indonesia, and after much research, the evidence pointed to the effectiveness of squatting to get the deed done. Yet, despite all the data, the modern toilet hasn't evolved in any material way.

Sure, it's a gross topic, but want to know what's even more disgusting? The average person walks around with five to ten pounds of shit in their body. Now, that's just plain nasty and debilitating. People are basically carrying a bag of garbage that slows them physically, mentally, and emotionally, but no one likes to talk about it. This natural human process is unavoidable and needs to be discussed without shame or embarrassment.

When I first dabbled in this space during my marriage to Monique, we decided on a fun and rather pricy vacation to perform an extended cleanse at the We Care Spa in Desert Hot Springs, California. For a week, I subsisted on green juices while receiving daily colonics and occasional massages to distract myself from the prolonged hunger pains. From my perspective, I saw this place as a bit of an absurdity because I paid top dollar to starve myself and get flushed out, all in the most austere space imaginable. Oh, and to top it off, no electronics. Sounds like fun, huh?

By day four, Monique had enough, and we packed up to head home from our "vacation." We were badgers on a night raid as the full-on sugar withdrawals compelled us to action. So, as good junkies, we found the closest grocery store and downed a whole box of cookies along with a large bag of M&Ms as we jammed to tunes on the drive back home. It felt good for about an hour. It was the worst decision after making an investment in our health . . . live and learn.

These days, I'm more methodical in my approach. I perform a five-day cleanse, a.k.a. exorcism, three times a year using a formula perfected by Dr. Schulze's. I also get colonics every three months and throw in an occasional home enema for good measure. I do all this because removing the body's trash makes me feel amazing. After this ordeal, my body shows gratitude through clearer vision, stronger taste buds, and boundless energy. Back to the car analogy, this is the body one gets for life, and changing the oil regularly leads to better performance.

I would be remiss if I didn't address water consumption since it's key to flushing my pipes and giving my body new life. I consume about one and a half gallons a day. If it gets boring, I spice it up with flavored electrolytes; Ultima orange or grape are my favorites. My body usually lets me know when I'm a quart or two low with feelings of lethargy, fogginess, or constipation. Ideally, I work to preempt these feelings, as once they hit, the body is already dehydrated.

Health is a quality-of-life decision. I chose health, and my dedication has kept me in the game. While there's certainly no right way, and life is ever-changing, I offer my experience and evolution as one of many paths for consideration.

While physical health has been a lifelong commitment, the complement of mental, spiritual, and emotional wellness has grown in focus over the last several decades. It's been challenging but rewarding work. And just like physical fitness, I won't stop, because I know it helps me become a better version of myself, more patient and compassionate than I am without it. In essence, it helps me be strong enough to be kind, especially when it's hard.

Naturally, I have concerns and a strong desire to keep my mind sharp after twenty-five years of head-banging football and a father who died of Alzheimer's disease. So, I work to keep mindlessness out of my home and replace it with exercising my brain and focusing on continuous learning. I ditched my television long ago, opting for educational documentaries, PBS, MasterClass, and TED Talks on my computer. I supplement this with a few Audible and Kindle books at any time. If all else fails, there are kangaroo fights on YouTube for the distractible days.

I found that my mental performance is highly affected by my spiritual and emotional training, which has also evolved. One unexpected influence on this path came from a chance encounter. It was fortuitous, given that I had just finished reading Tony Robbins's

Awaken the Giant Within when I bumped into him at a Los Angeles Kings game. We exchanged pleasantries, and I invited him to the next Raiders game, not fully recognizing the door I was opening. As I checked out the stands before taking the field five days later, I was pleased to watch Tony and his son pointing around the field with big smiles and carrying on like a tight-knit father and son as fans surrounding them were transfixed. Even from a distance, I could see that there was something special about Tony. He was a magnet that attracted everyone to him, not just because of his celebrity status, oversized stature, or booming voice.... There were plenty of those types taking the field that morning. It was something else I would come to understand in time.

Not long after, Tony cajoled me into my first fire walk. The premise behind the exercise is that anything is possible if you just get started and keep moving. Given how I approached life, this should've been easy. I remember walking up to the smoldering coals and taking a step back as I confronted a wall of heat that enveloped me like an inescapable gauze. The coals were cherry red and uninviting.

"You got this, Steve, no sweat," Tony bellowed and waved his large hands toward the end of the pathway. It was the first time I noticed his hands, which was remarkable, given their massive size. For years, people joked about my handshake feeling like grabbing a bunch of bananas. But, to me, they were a gift on the offensive line and came in handy working in the trench. Tony could've palmed helmets with those mitts. This thought distracted me enough to reflexively step forward as he ushered me into the walk.

I narrowed my eyes as I stepped my bare feet onto the path of red-hot coals while I fixed my gaze skyward and tried to ignore the embers wafting through the air. Just like in life, getting started was the hard part, and I made it to the end of the line before I had a chance to think.

"What did I tell you? It was easier than a game, right?" Tony flashed his larger-than-life smile with perfect pearly whites. His charisma was effortless.

"Thanks for the nudge. I needed that," I admitted, bending down to check for embers stuck between my toes.

"Now that that's out of the way, come with me up to Minneapolis for the NBA all-star game," he offered as I realized that this man had boundless energy and the resources to match.

So, I joined Tony on his plane for a whirlwind two-night trip where I barely saw my hotel room. The man doesn't sleep. Instead, his unrelenting quest to help others compels him day and night. This gave him a remarkable authenticity when he engaged with anyone, known or unknown to him. I witnessed it firsthand as we left the stadium after the game. Like the brutal winters of my childhood, the winds in Minneapolis blew drifts in all directions, and visibility was low. A block off the stadium, we happened across a homeless man resting in a high snowdrift just off the walkway. Tony plopped into the drift beside him and began chatting. Like everyone else who encountered Tony, the man took to him right away and poured out his life story, hopes, and dreams. After about fifteen minutes, Tony pulled off his scarf and gloves and offered them as gifts. As the man politely declined, Tony discreetly slipped a couple of one-hundred-dollar bills into the gloves and placed them on the man's lap when he stood to depart.

As we were turning to leave, he bent down to connect his eyes with the man once again and whispered something in his ear. The man smiled and nodded with a deep appreciation visible in his eyes. Whatever Tony said, the man felt seen and valued.

A block later, I turned to him. "I've just got to know. What did you say to that guy before we left? Because whatever it was, you did something special that I haven't seen in quite a while," I confessed.

Tony nodded. "I told him that he was me."

"What do you mean?" I asked.

"Well, I lived on the streets before I made it, so I know how cruel life can be out here. I wanted him to know that I deeply understand the challenges he faces daily. I am him, and he is me," he stated, then nodded and kept walking.

It wasn't until decades later that I came across a concept that embodied his parting comment that night. The African philosophy of Ubuntu encapsulates it best: I am because you are. It's in the act of offering your humanity to others that you become undeniably human and connected. I was offered powerful models and reminders to shine my light on others through years of consistently observing Gramps and Dad, as well as this powerful experience with Tony.

I'm sad to admit that I never drew this connection through my experiences with the church. As a kid, I was dragged to a Presbyterian church where worship never felt authentic to me. We wore our coat and ties, smiled, and left it all in the pews when the service was over. There was never a word of God or a prayer at our house, and I have a pretty good feeling that was the case for most of the congregation.

I also led the military ministry at Mariners Church in Newport Beach for several years. I thrived on the challenge of increasing our volunteer base because our mission was so pure: to support the families of US Marines based out of Camp Pendleton. "Believe" was the basic call sign to stay focused, but it was eye-opening to see how many volunteers lacked faith or belief in our mission.

I finally put down my Bible when my men's group spoke more about their homes, cars, and hotties than the word of God. It made my stomach churn. Perhaps my situation was unique, but mounting concerns drove me elsewhere to fill my spiritual cup.

My current path began with the integration of meditation over a decade ago with Grant Mattos after our stint on reality TV. I discovered that waking and turning inward during my morning gave me energy, focus, and even more positivity to feed my day. As my guru, Sadhguru, explained, "Meditation isn't about going somewhere—it is falling back into yourself." It reinforces who I want to be as I meditate using mantras to guide my karmic life. I know the good and bad will return to me, and I actively choose good. Since our life here is short, I want to shine with positivity and spread it wide.

Sometimes my mantras are more basic than Gandhi's *Be the Change*. I'll focus on listening to others, or more accurately, not reacting before carefully considering their words. An intentional focus on nonreaction serves me, as a quick retort rarely resolves conflict. It's important to me that people feel heard and respected because, as Maya Angelou so accurately describes, "People will forget what you said, people will forget what you did, but people will never forget how you made them feel."

While meditation is a central practice of Buddhism, my journey to fully embrace this spiritual path was a slower, more thoughtful process. At first, I was weary of any label, but eventually, Buddhism felt so right and natural to me that I didn't want to deny it. Unlike some other doctrines, it focuses inward, thereby becoming very personal. I hold myself accountable that I alone am responsible for my well-being. In a world where we lack so much control, this is powerful stuff.

I went all in, pouring over the wisdom of great souls such as Thích Nhất Hạnh and the Dalai Lama, whom I admire, but from afar, as many of their teachings still felt outside my grasp. Yet they opened my heart and eyes, so when the light shined on the right path for me, I walked straight toward what I had been seeking all along.

I was listening to my friend's podcast while doing the morning dishes when his guest, Sadhguru, caught my attention. I immediately put the plates down, turned off the water, and grabbed my notebook. I was transfixed. I was attracted to his logical and practical articulations as opposed to other great thinkers' lofty and sometimes perplexing words. Sadhguru was relatable, humble, and humorous—my kind of guy.

Sadhguru is a yogi, a mystic, and a real man who rides his motorcycle all over the world on a quest to share his wisdom. He garners respect speaking to the elite at the United Nations, Oxford, and Harvard, but he spends most of his time touching the masses. He offers compelling thoughts on every topic imaginable, from self-discipline to self-doubt and digestion as he peppers personal stories and jokes into his messages. He has many powerful sayings, but one deeply resonates with my approach to life: "Do not worry about setting goals for yourself—just see how to constantly grow. All that is needed is relentless striving to be a full-fledged self."

One of my greatest acts of self-love came at the urging of my guru, who encouraged freeing my being from negativity. It hasn't always been easy to distance myself from people living in a negative headspace, but it's been necessary to maintain my joy. I learned not to work to change others or justify my path, as we all need to walk our own way. Better to wish them well than waste precious time.

My greatest teacher in this regard, however, wasn't my guru. It was my brother, Dave. I spent many years struggling with this relationship as we attempted to develop our Iowa property. We always got along well on the easy stuff like family trips or holidays, primarily because my family excelled at keeping the topics of conversation light. It wasn't until we bumped up against business decisions that the friction became obvious and overwhelming. Yet, with the benefit of much reflection, I suspect the tension lay dormant because of our starkly different upbringings.

Dave and I would yell at each other, with neither one listening nor seeking to understand. The stalemate was like having old milk in the refrigerator, and eventually, it became unbearable for everyone around us. As the stink mounted, our efforts to manipulate became more poisonous. We went from lighthearted conversations to all-out verbal assaults, pulling in family bystanders to watch in disgust. Finally, I could no longer handle the negativity coming from him or myself and walked away cold turkey, leaving a sister as a casualty of family war. It took all I could manage to stifle my ego and exit stage left, but the relationship was going from bad to worse. I recognized that a part of me needed some more introspection and inner engineering. It was time to walk away and work on myself through my spiritual practice.

Letting go doesn't just apply to people; it's included decluttering my whole environment to eliminate negativity and create more space for joy. For example, do I need a new computer, or do I just *want* the latest and greatest model? I run everything through this assessment, from buying a home to cars, pets, and even my clothes, and I make sure that *need* rules the day.

It sounds simple, but in practice, it involves some trade-offs, self-discipline, and disregard for status considerations. I rent a 700-square-foot apartment with only the bare minimum of furniture because I need a place to live, but I also love to travel and detest home maintenance. When I lived in a 6,500-square-foot luxurious cliffside estate, the entire space felt negative . . . beautiful, but the proverbial gilded cage nonetheless. While there are advantages to home ownership, I decided that some things are more important than money. As Plato asserted, "The greatest wealth is to live content with little." So, when you see a big guy driving around Malibu in an old BMW wearing swim trunks, beat-up old sunglasses, and a big smile on his face, there's a good chance that it's me.

The smile has been there throughout my life, but there were a few times when I needed help recapturing the joy. As my first marriage began to unravel, we sought out couples therapy. Not knowing much about different modalities, our first attempt involved a recommended psychotherapist who was a huge disappointment, but it was a learning experience.

Her office was the classic Laguna Beach setup. All beachy and breezy, with well-appointed furniture, classy art, and tasteful accent pillows on several beautifully upholstered chairs. I frowned as I thought about our master bedroom when I saw the pillows. I kid you not; Monique had over a dozen on our bed. I wanted to toss them, but I didn't need to start any more trivial arguments with our marriage already fragile. As we approached the couch staged for clients, I parted the sea and sat while Monique stood nearby, scanning the room with a touch of admiration shining through her expression.

"Such a beautiful space," Monique said, eyeing the art above and the pillows engulfing me.

"Ah, thanks. I tried to make it feel like a home," the therapist said, shifting her Hermes belt buckle.

"It's lovely," Monique commented with a tone I knew well. She meant it; she was digging this space.

Eager to get past the small talk, I waited for Monique to finally take a seat on the other end of the couch, affixing my gaze on our ringleader. The therapist sensed my desire to begin the session and nodded as she took her position across from us in an ivory armchair.

"Steve, why don't you start with how you are feeling?" she asked as she raised her brows to signal the start of the clock, or so I assumed.

"I feel sad about where we are today," I said, looking lovingly into Monique's eyes. She had the most amazing big green eyes that revealed her soulfulness. I was still very much in love with her and knew it was worth working to save what we had built. I didn't wait until I was forty to get married and bail without a fight to save it.

"How does that make you feel?" the therapist interjected, her neck craning toward Monique.

"I'm sad, too, of course, but this isn't working," she responded with obvious strain and exhaustion. Looking closely, I could see the fine lines under her eyes, pulling at the beauty she radiated and dampening her vibrancy.

"What do you think about what Monique has shared, Steve?" the therapist said as she swiveled her neck to peer in my direction while I continued to examine my love.

After a long pause, I looked back at the therapist. I wanted to say something sarcastic, but I didn't need to be the bad guy two minutes into this session. Yet I couldn't resist the urge to contort my head and extend my neck like a telescope toward the therapist, saying, "What do you think?" I suspected that my tone revealed my frustration with the session's trajectory. Trying to recover, I continued, "I mean, don't you think it's appropriate for both of us to be sad?"

"I'm here to help you discover your feelings, Steve, not mine," she said with calm and unaffected speech as she crossed her bony ankles and tightened her grip on an ivory pen.

It was clear that we weren't with the right therapist. Since it was a small town, and people talked, I played nice for the rest of the session, but mentally, I kept count of the number of questions the therapist numbly tossed into the mix to stir things up. We left the session with a basket full of questions and no path or answers to guide us out of this dark tunnel. We tried several more therapists, but nothing worked, and after ten years joined at the hip, we had no choice but to lovingly part ways.

In the aftermath, I found a cognitive therapist who made a significant difference in my life during a period of intense vulnerability. Surprisingly, I didn't require many sessions because the solution-minded therapeutic approach suited my coachable nature. I appreciated the homework, and unlike my time in school, I took it to heart. It worked so well for processing my divorce that we covered other sensitive topics too, including my relationship with my son and siblings. There was also some free therapy that I took advantage of daily: my sunrise beach runs. I can't recall how many things I processed and worked through on those early runs, but it's substantial. The rhythmic movement, silence, sun, and healing breeze all contributed to countless moments of enlightenment over the decades.

Another part of my emotional growth included finding ways to get outside myself and give back. Through nothing but the luck of the draw, I was delivered into an upper-middle-class family that gave me a leg up in all regards. My sensitivity to inequities began at age ten when Dad's company gifted us a family country-club membership intended to groom clients. It was a bastion of upper-class White families attended to by less fortunate Black and Hispanic workers. I was little enough to remain inconspicuous and watched the interactions with great interest. In those hallways and fairways, I witnessed the good and bad in humanity as they either embraced or mistreated the staff.

With eleven more years of growing and observing others, I landed in Dallas, ready to do more. My good fortune was only increasing while the inequities around me were mounting. It started in the offseason when the Cowboys' front office reached out for volunteers. The opportunities ranged from visiting youth homes and special hospitals to feeding the homeless. My involvement increased when I landed in Los Angeles, where I found myself spread too thin with more fundraising golf tournaments than I could count. I was sent on plenty of boondoggles as well. The worst was a fundraising Bun Run at a nudist camp. It was a foul couple of hours watching unsightly naked people running for a local charity. Rest assured that I'll never set foot in a nudist colony again, no matter how much money we could raise. Some things can't be unseen.

There was one act of giving that truly stood out during my time in Los Angeles due to the scale of the undertaking and its impact. While seeking donations for the Marine Corps, I had the good fortune of meeting the owner of the behemoth Hyatt Regency Huntington Beach Resort and Spa over lunch. Not mincing words, he offered a generous gift. Did I want every piece of furniture in the 574-room hotel, including beds, couches, desks, lamps, and chairs for any Marine Corps families in need? I was floored and said yes before I could assess the magnitude of the effort. There was one significant catch, though: all the rooms' contents needed to be removed within two weeks, as the hotel's new furniture and decor was already on order. If I didn't get to it fast, customers would buy the used stuff in a heartbeat.

With the help of many Marines with monster trucks, discipline, and plenty of manpower, the teams worked to get it all out within a week and a half. It was such a pleasure working with these highly efficient and mission-driven soldiers. We worked from a massive spreadsheet with alternative plans at the ready but remarkably didn't encounter any significant obstacles. It was impossible to describe the incredible gift of watching these hardworking Marine Corps families light up over the goods that help turn their houses into homes. While there's always more that can be done, it was rewarding to show gratitude for all their sacrifices, seen and unseen, that keep us safe.

Another charity experience left me wondering if I was helpful to the cause. Despite being a below-average golfer, I played in plenty of tournaments over the years for camaraderie and to raise money for great causes. I was playing in my sixth Long Beach Celebrity Grand Prix Golf Tournament with great stars and athletes from various sports.

The shotgun went off, signaling the start of the tournament. My team wanted me to tee off first, a decision they soon regretted. It was 9 a.m., and we had plenty of onlookers to watch the big man swing, so I let it rip. I hit a low smoking ball that sliced right and then a little further right as it climbed. It was headed straight for a clump of bushes that protected another tee box, so I yelled "fore" as loud as possible to warn the golfers to cover up since my ball was beelining in their direction. The ball was still rising and picking up speed as it vanished into the bush and sounded like it hit a coconut from one hundred yards away. My gut was screaming that I hit someone, and my mind was pleading, *No, please, no.*

I ran off the tee to get a better angle and saw everyone kneeling around a body. I dropped my club and sprinted to find a man holding a rag to his face. I took a quick inventory: he still had both eyes, but the rag on his forehead was full of blood. Then I noticed something hard to unsee . . . he was a unicorn. My ball landed dead center on his forehead, and the lump was still expanding outward as it split his skin. Fortunately, he was awake and heard the club assistant call for an ambulance.

"No way, I'm playing. I'm okay," he said, far more concerned about golf than his new horn.

I was feeling relieved before the celebrity in their group, Olympian Bruce Jenner, piped up. "This is what happens when you have these football players here."

I knew Bruce from a commercial we shot together a few years back, but I wasn't going to put up with his cheap shot. "Shut your mouth. This is no joke," I said as I grit my teeth and used my size to get in his face and call him off.

Bruce could tell I wasn't amused and kept quiet, other than to mumble, "Okay, man, relax."

I felt horrible not only for accidentally hurting someone but for not bringing my best self into the equation in the aftermath. In the end, though, the unicorn enjoyed a full day of golf with the best story, and I never got invited back to the tournament. While this door humbled me, it also reinforced my desire and, quite frankly, my need to bring my best self wherever I go and in whatever I do. Yes, things will happen that I don't expect, but it's in the reaction and treatment of others that I make amends. I needed a reminder, and the Grand Prix Golf Tournament delivered.

With so many charity opportunities offered up, it became hard to say no. But, after the Bun Run experience and my disaster on the golf course, I started filtering my choices through the lens of impact. Where could I do the most good? As a result, I now dive deeper into a cause to understand the matrix behind the public front. I focus all my effort on Globall Giving. The cause allows me to bring sports to kids in need to tackle health, wellness, and inequity. As an athlete, I know full well what sports can do to change the life trajectory of a kid. Whether White, Black, Asian, or other—of wealth or poverty—the field of opportunity is boundless.

CHAPTER 9

FLOW LIKE WATER

I can't fully address physical, mental, spiritual, and emotional health without tackling the inevitable: aging and death. I watched plenty of people fight the laws of nature, like water going uphill. Meanwhile, others resigned themselves to decline and slowly wasted away. And then there were the handful of wise sages who flowed like water. They didn't resist or submit but instead charted a new course. These were the ones who inspired me.

When I hit my mid-fifties, I became acutely aware of guys who challenged the flow. I first noticed them in the gym. They had something to prove as they grabbed the heaviest weights and fought through pain. I lost count of the torn biceps, strained shoulders and wrists, and popped tendons I witnessed as guys took on Father Time in front of the weight bench and mirror. Invariably, they may have won a few battles but always lost the war.

Their debilitating injuries were just the visible manifestations of their struggle. Something far more sinister rattled below the surface as their sense of well-being was upended. From what I observed, being at odds with nature was a surefire path to physical and emotional pain. But thanks to football, this route was avoidable. I had twenty-five years of listening and learning from my body to prevent career-ending injuries, and I discovered that these well-honed instincts didn't turn off in retirement. The "don't be stupid" alarm bell was alive and well, saving me plenty of pain.

Another group gave up altogether as they detached from the natural flow. With youth a distant memory, they offered the old "screw off" to life. The physical signs of these journeymen were the easiest to spot. Any self-care was a lost art, and physical fitness was off the radar. Feeling crappy was the new normal as they slowly faded away. It was an unfortunate way to live out the last part of life, yet it is far too common. After my divorce, I fell into this resigned state. I hated how my energy waned and my waistline expanded as I got a little too comfortable with my daily patterns and my nightly desserts. Fortunately, I self-corrected before it got too out of hand, but it was a good reminder to stay vigilant.

Then there were those who flowed like water. They bowed to the wisdom of Bruce Lee when he said, "Be like water making its way through cracks. Do not be assertive, but adjust to the object, and you shall find a way around or through it. If nothing within you stays rigid, outward things will disclose themselves." Now these devotees, from what I observed, had this aging thing figured out. They understood the river would never flow backward, so fighting it was useless. However, they weren't resigned to a particular fate. They treated life as an endless set of possibilities, letting their water flow on its course, adjusting, and evolving as they aged. When joints got stiff, they picked up yoga or traded in a few weightlifting days for stretching. They didn't seem to be afraid of these adjustments, and so, given my options, I worked on flowing like water.

I'm far from having it all figured out, but inspired by this path, I view aging, and especially death, as the next adventure. While I'm in no hurry to move on, I recognize that everything here is impermanent. My mind, heart, and affairs are clear and organized, which helps me live fully, love completely, and bring positivity to everything I do. It'll also help me depart with ease when it's time. Yes, it's painstaking to do all the legal work of trusts, health directives, and wills, but they're essential to my peace of mind.

My one and only brush with death was a reminder to embrace

life. I was vacationing in Lake Powell for a week to enjoy some boating with friends. Midway through our stay, I decided to take one of the speedboats to grab a few things from the marina. As I punched it to make good time, my buddy forgot to lift the tri-hook anchor securing the boat. This ride had a ridiculous amount of power as my speed quickly hit forty miles per hour. Meanwhile, I had no idea the anchor was bouncing around behind this speed machine like a tool of death poising to strike.

Suddenly, there was a deafening bang, followed by something wrapping around me, igniting a fierce burning sensation. There was nothing out in front of me that I hit, so I couldn't make sense of the noose wrapping around me with such ferocity. I scrambled to throw it into neutral, and within seconds, the boat was coasting as I fell on all fours spitting blood. I got lucky that day because the anchor flew by my head, breaking the windshield on its way past before it bounced off the front and back into the water. As I examined my body, I found that the anchor's rope buzzed off the front of my gums while my forearm absorbed the brunt of the force. My buddy looked on in awe at the whole scene. I guess it just wasn't my time, but it was enough of a reminder to get my affairs in order should the unexpected strike.

As Sadhguru wisely explained, "Karma means ultimate responsibility. You even take responsibility for your very birth and death." I feel disheartened for the millions of older adults who aren't allowed to leave when they choose. Most have managed a wonderful life directing all their decisions but then face laws forbidding them from departing on their terms. I experienced this with my father, who went from the happiest man to being stricken with Alzheimer's disease. When it hit, he was seventy-three years old, and it jumped on him hard.

When my father was diagnosed, neither parent acknowledged nor openly addressed the disease. This was a consistent theme with unpleasant news throughout my upbringing, but the consequences of their intentional ignorance were dire in this case. I recall being in the doctor's office with my parents when they learned of the diagnosis. I was furious with the doctor for not naming it Alzheimer's but instead calling it Dad's condition. This was music to the ears of these two, who were perfectly willing to go on pretending everything was fine. Just as when I told Mom about the unplanned pregnancy, her reaction was for us to go to lunch and discuss the pastrami sandwiches instead of the disease killing my father.

Only one year later, Dad confided in me. "I can feel my mind going," he said as he cringed. He was eager for someone to "help me leave," he said, but he was going too fast. I firmly believe he was ready to pass on but instead endured disorientation, incapacitation, and pervasive fear for another several years. I can still picture his frightened face before he died. It remains the strongest, most painful memory of my father. But instead of dwelling on his end, I chose to focus on the amazing influence he had on my life. Because of him, I consistently chose happiness, assumed the best, led with kindness, and insisted that anything was possible. This was his legacy and his most incredible gift to me.

I hope to pay it forward as Dad did for me. When in this state, the universe becomes a bastion of opportunity, and things I never even imagined came my way. This was my experience joining former astronaut Buzz Aldrin to float in zero gravity at Zero-G in Nevada. It was a memorable day in many regards, but the most wonderful part was observing Buzz, who laughed and danced in zero gravity like an unattended child in a candy shop. I didn't know then, but this was his first return to zero gravity since landing on the moon in 1969.

We met in the Nevada desert, where we were the only things moving beyond the tumbleweeds bouncing along the desert floor. Buzz caught my attention immediately because he couldn't wipe the huge grin off his face, and his foot tapped in anticipation of our takeoff. He was a spitfire, ready to get back into space or the closest he could come within our atmosphere.

We were provided jumpsuits and training on managing the fifteen parabolic arcs needed to achieve rounds of zero gravity. The plane was a modified Boeing 727 in its own airspace called "The Playground" that spanned one hundred miles. This roller-coaster ride began between 24,000 to 32,000 feet, offering weightlessness lasting thirty seconds. At the peak, the plane dove sharply, lifting us off the floor, and the fun commenced.

Looking around me during periods of weightlessness, I watched Buzz drink floating water bubbles and toss M&Ms in my direction. He was the embodiment of pure joy.

"Steve, let me spin you around!" he said, barreling in my direction with a mouthful of M&Ms.

He didn't wait for my response as he grabbed my jumpsuit and gave me a twirl. As I floated back around, I met his eyes, which sparkled with the joy that only comes from being fully absorbed in the present.

"I've missed this feeling," he said, waving his arms toward the sky. "I miss everything about that experience." His voice trailed off as he spoke more to the universe than to me.

"Would you go back?" I asked, rhetorically, of course, as his retirement stood as the logical barrier to spaceflight at his age.

"I wouldn't hesitate for a second," he said just as we disengaged from zero gravity and landed back on our feet.

My time with Buzz was a powerful reminder that passion keeps us young. It might not reverse inevitable physical aging, but it can keep the spirit ageless.

Zero G

CHAPTER 10

FORWARD MOMENTUM

The universe works in mysterious ways. At the last Raiders reunion, guess who took the seat next to me? Killer.

Henry Lawrence sauntered up to the table dressed beyond the occasion in black leather pants and a sleek shirt hugging his formidable body. Even in the company of former athletes, he stood out. Despite the aging of time, his eyes were a dead giveaway as he scanned the crowd with a familiar intensity. He was getting his game face on, but for what?

His movement was smooth with the unmistakable confidence of an apex predator as he slid into the booth and waited for me to engage. I vowed not to fumble my words like our last interaction on the Raiders picket line. That conversation was a mere week before I took his job and ended his illustrious career. I had no idea if he harbored a grudge.

I kept the conversation light as I leaned in and hoped to charm him with a warm smile and a strong fist bump. Much to my surprise, his eyes, while still dilated in anticipation of something game-worthy, softened. He cracked a side smile, signaling that the past was put to rest. We caught up about old colleagues and life after football, but all the while, I sensed that his mind was on something more pressing.

As we filled our plates at the buffet in the field-level suite, I watched Henry mound his plate with vegetables instead of the steak and crab legs at our disposal. He talked about healthy eating, staying positive, and an unwavering commitment to his community. As it turns out, we had more in common in retirement than during our playing days. Yet, just as he finished, he rose and vanished. He left so fast that I wondered if I had said something to offend him.

Ten minutes later, a familiar voice filled the stadium. It was Henry. I looked to the jumbotron to see him mic'd with a full band filling out center stage. He launched into a popular soul song with a deep velvety voice that got a crowd of 65,000 fans singing along. He was a natural, and his light was shining bright.

All the time we were chatting, he was preparing to perform the way he readied for games so many years ago. But now he was channeling his love, not his killer instincts. The widest smile came to my face as I lifted my fist into the air and whistled. Henry triumphed in life beyond the field when he achieved a healthy balance. While his football career ended abruptly, he found God, became a pastor, and poured his heart into a singing career. He was living his dream, and I got to see it.

It was a beautiful moment and reinforced my conviction that society's definition of masculinity needs to expand to make space for both aggression and empathy. They're fundamental parts of being a healthy, well-adjusted man. The real key, which took me nearly a lifetime to learn, is knowing when and how to engage them to make life better for myself and those around me. And much like the Eastern concepts of yin and yang, one cannot exist without the other. I have darkness and light, aggression and empathy, and the list goes on. They're all within, forever sliding across the spectrum based on life and circumstances. As quantum mechanics suggests, nothing in existence is static. Even in their lowest possible state, particles have zero-point energy. So, everything is moving, sliding, and becoming . . . all part of this crazy universal dance.

My journey to navigate conflicting characteristics and become more fully human has been a wonderfully wild ride. While it took nearly half a century and more than my fair share of defining experiences, I remain a traveler on the journey of learning to become my best self. It may seem counterintuitive, but the process of going inward after football expanded me outwardly. That's why the concept of Ubuntu resonates so deeply for me: I've become more fully human through the act of offering my light to others, like Henry to his church.

On a grander scale, imagine what collective mastery of our darkness and light could mean for the world. Shared empathy, paired with action, is already propelling us in the right direction as this next generation makes meaningful progress. They combine their compassion with innovative thinking, employing technology to garner attention and establish new solutions. They freely challenge conventional truisms, boldly stepping outside the lines. Unlike those before them, they aren't constrained by the assembly line and groupthink. I'm convinced they will be our salvation.

Driven by their commitment, I'm excited to see positive environmental solutions gaining mainstream attention, with progress occurring at a faster pace than ever before. Much-needed desalination plants are popping up worldwide, with over 18,000 delivering potable water to those in need. Meat production is in decline, reducing environmental hazards, with more choosing a plant-based diet. And fortunately, solar and wind energy are finding their footing. It's become part of the global consciousness to do more to save the planet. This gives me hope that someday an individual's small carbon footprint will be more of a status symbol than any product.

Meanwhile, young activists are using wide-ranging platforms to speak out and raise awareness of social injustices that require visibility and steadfast dedication to change. Their grit, determination, and sacrifice are moving the needle on race, gender, and sexual orientation. Company boards are changing, sports participation is broadening, and conventional norms about gender are expanding while exclusionary policies gather dust. We're all 99.9 percent genetically identical. Why let artificial divisions persist?

While there's much more to do, this next generation is relentlessly committed. I share in their dedication and will never stop striving to be aggressively human. Because as Desmond Tutu wisely explained, "My humanity is bound up in yours, for we can only be human together."

So, yes, I am Killer. And Killer is me. But we are both so much more than that. It's only a part of what makes us wholly human. This realization struck me at the reunion. I had spent my early years embracing aggression, just like Henry. It was the ultimate job security. And when we met on the field for the first time, there was no way that I could fully see him. And I suspect the inverse was true as well. I had decades of inside work ahead that was necessary for growth. I'm guessing that Henry did, too.

Once I learned how to navigate my aggression and empathy, I could appreciate Henry for more than just Killer. Likewise, he could see me more completely. The transition from inside work to outside acknowledgment allowed me to recognize our intertwined humanity. I have the concept of Ubuntu to thank for articulating this universal truth. I share my thoughts in hopes of encouraging others to chart their unique path toward a world in which we fully see each other and are strong enough to be kind.

ACKNOWLEDGMENTS

The period spent writing this memoir was one of the best of my life. It shouldn't have been, given that the pandemic was raging around me and life after lockdown was anything but certain. Yet, for eight straight months, I thrived in a cocoon of reflection that brought unmatched joy to my life as I unearthed memories and reconnected with old teammates and friends to confirm my account of events.

I rose each morning thinking about different life experiences, often with a big smile, as the majority of my life has been a source of amusement and positivity. After typing up an event or two, I would surf the web to validate details before a nightly meeting with Lizzy. We would dissect the content, rewrite, and polish pieces like a dishwashing machine stuck on rinse. Some nights, we would laugh, and others were red-pen bloodbaths, but all the massaging made the end product something I am proud of. I learned so much about the writing process through MasterClasses, YouTube videos, books, and websites dedicated to the craft. I even attended a book conference, where I wandered like a gorilla in a birdcage, but I pressed on like a navigator in a new land.

There are so many people to thank for their contributions and support, but one name stands above the rest . . . Lizzy. She insisted that there was something to my handling of aggression and empathy that was worthy of sharing, as she saw both a rottweiler and golden retriever resting comfortably within. Her unceasing support and drive gave the work life and shaped an unparalleled gift I will always treasure.

Neil Strauss, one in my workout tribe, who just happens to be a ten-time *New York Times* best-selling author, was another light in the tunnel. He took this newbie under his wing and boiled a career of experience down to bite-sized wisdom and feedback as I navigated the brave new world of writing.

My old teammates offered their encouragement as well, with special thanks to Steve Beuerlein, Eric Dickerson, Tony Dorsett, Chris Hinton, Howie Long, and Howard Richards. Their collective memories brought even more color to many of the events that shaped me during my time in the NFL.

To my publisher, Koehler Books, led by John Koehler and his exceptional team of professionals, thank you for seeing the possibility in my work. You have been an absolute dream partner on the publishing journey. And to Ziv Fisher at 48 Windows, I am forever thankful for your patience and expertise in delivering an audible product befitting the work. I also had the great fortune to learn from one of the best, actor and good friend John C. McGinley, who went above and beyond to school me.

And finally, to you, the reader: thank you for your time. It's the most precious gift you could offer, and I am forever grateful that you stuck with me. And now, onto the next chapter of this crazy ride, where I plan to jump into the first seats of the roller coaster and embrace whatever manifests, as there is nothing greater than to enjoy the journey.

REFERENCES

Cloudburst. "Cloudburst Misting Systems." Accessed July 1, 2023. https://cloudburst.com.

Community Tsunami Museum. "Community Tsunami Museum and Education Center Hikkaduwa." Accessed July 1, 2023. https://southernsrilanka.lk/attractions/museums-2-2.

Courtesy 180. "Courtesy 180." YouTube, June 17, 2021. https://www.youtube.com/watch?v=CWJeA6YqVWo.

Dr. Schulze's. "My 5 Steps to Change Your Life." Accessed July 1, 2023. https://www.herbdoc.com.

Dwyre, Bill. "A 'real lucky' former NFL player irked by progress on concussions and injuries." *Los Angeles Times*, October 2, 2015.

Globall Giving. "Our Mission." Accessed July 1, 2023. https://globallgiving.org.

Huizenga, Robert MD. You're Okay, It's Just a Bruise: A Doctor's Sideline Secrets About Pro Football's Most Outrageous Team. New York: St. Martin's Griffin, 1994.

Pence, Laila. "Pence Wealth Management." Accessed July 1, 2023. https://pencewealthmanagement.com.

PFC Nutrition. "Performance Fitness Concepts." Accessed July 1, 2023. https://www.pfcnutrition.com.

Philips, Bill and Michael D'Orso. Body for Life: 12 Weeks to Mental and Physical Strength. New York: HarperCollins, 1999.

Robbins, Anthony. Awaken the Giant Within: How to Take Immediate Control of Your Mental, Emotional, Physical and Financial Destiny! New York: Simon & Schuster, 1992.

Sadhguru. "Isha." Accessed July 1, 2023. https://isha.sadhguru.org/us.en.

Therabody. "Therabody." Accessed July 1, 2023. https://www.therabody.com.

Printed in the USA
CPSIA information can be obtained
at www.ICGtesting.com
LVHW042045021223
765141LV00056B/889